Brief Contents

Foundations First

Sentences and Paragraphs

WITH READINGS

FOURTH EDITION

Foundations First
Sentences and Paragraphs

WITH READINGS

Laurie G. Kirszner

University of the Sciences

Stephen R. Mandell

Drexel University

Bedford/St. Martin's

Boston ◆ New York

For Bedford/St. Martin's

Senior Developmental Editor: Ellen Darion
Senior Production Editor: William Imbornoni
Senior Production Supervisor: Nancy J. Myers
Senior Marketing Manager: Christina Shea
Art Director: Lucy Krikorian
Text Design: Claire Seng-Niemoeller
Photo Research: Susan Doheny
Permissions Manager: Kalina K. Ingham
Cover Design: Donna Lee Dennison
Cover Art: Gaze Quartet by Susannah Bielak, courtesy of the artist
Composition: Graphic World, Inc.
Printing and Binding: RR Donnelley & Sons

President: Joan E. Feinberg
Editorial Director: Denise B. Wydra
Editor in Chief: Karen S. Henry
Director of Development: Erica T. Appel
Director of Marketing: Karen R. Soeltz
Director of Production: Susan W. Brown
Associate Director, Editorial Production: Elise S. Kaiser
Managing Editor: Shuli Traub

Library of Congress Control Number: 2011931593

Manufactured in the United States of America.

6   5   4   3   2   1
f   e   d   c   b   a

For information, write: Bedford/St. Martin's, 75 Arlington Street, Boston, MA 02116   (617-399-4000)

ISBN: 978-0-312-60318-2 (Instructor's Annotated Edition)
ISBN: 978-0-312-60316-8 (Student Edition)

Acknowledgments

Acknowledgments and copyrights appear at the back of the book on pages 625–26, which constitute an extension of the copyright page.

Preface for Instructors

We believe that in college, writing comes first and that students learn writing skills most meaningfully in the context of their own writing. For this reason, *Foundations First with Readings: Sentences and Paragraphs,* like our paragraph-to-essay text *Writing First,* takes a "practice in context" approach, teaching students the skills they need to become better writers by having them practice in the context of their own writing.

Equally important, *Foundations First* includes not just grammar and writing help but also a collection of invaluable resources to prepare developmental students for college work. By offering unique coverage of study skills, vocabulary building, ESL issues, and critical reading, *Foundations First* provides the support and encouragement students need to build a solid foundation for success in college and beyond.

In *Foundations First,* as in the classroom and in everyday life, writing is essential. For this reason, we begin with thorough coverage of the writing process. Most chapters begin with a Seeing and Writing prompt that asks students to respond in writing to a visual. Throughout the book, students learn to become better writers by applying each chapter's concepts to writing, revising, and editing their own responses to this prompt.

We wrote this book for adults—our own interested, concerned, and hardworking students—and we tailored the book's approach and content to them. Instead of exercises that reinforce the preconception that writing is a dull, pointless, and artificial activity, we chose fresh, contemporary examples (both student and professional) and developed interesting exercises and writing assignments. Throughout *Foundations First,* we talk *to* students, not *at* or *down* to them. We try to be concise without being abrupt, thorough without being repetitive, direct without being rigid, specific without being prescriptive, and flexible without being inconsistent. Our most important goal is simple: to create an engaging text that motivates students and gives students the tools and encouragement they need to improve their writing.

Organization

Foundations First with Readings: Sentences and Paragraphs has a flexible organization that enables instructors to teach topics in the order that works best for their students. The book opens with Unit One, which focuses on academic survival skills. This unit includes study skills, time management tips, readings strategies, and other practical advice to help students succeed in college. Unit Two provides a comprehensive discussion of the writing process, with chapters on all the major patterns of development and a full chapter on writing essays. Units Three through Six focus on sentence skills, grammar, punctuation, mechanics, and spelling. Unit Seven, Learning College Reading Skills, includes seventeen essays (three by student writers) accompanied by study questions and writing prompts. Finally, two appendixes, "Building Word Power" and "Strategies for Workplace Success," help students to master the vocabulary highlighted in the text and to prepare for real-world job situations.

For instructors wishing to emphasize the patterns of development, an Index of Rhetorical Patterns identifies essays and paragraphs that illustrate particular modes. (All of the patterns are covered in Unit 2, Chapters 5-13, and the essays in Unit Seven include at least one example of each pattern.)

Features

When we wrote *Foundations First*, our goal was to create the most useful and student-friendly sentence-to-paragraph text available for developmental writers. In preparing the fourth edition, we retained all the features that instructors told us contributed to the book's accessibility and effectiveness.

A complete resource for improving student writing. With one comprehensive unit on paragraphs, two units on sentences, two on grammar, one on reading, and numerous examples of student writing, *Foundations First* provides comprehensive coverage of basic writing in a format that gives instructors maximum flexibility in planning their courses.

"Writing in Context" writing activities. A multi-step *Seeing and Writing* strand in most chapters enables students to write, revise, and edit their own work from the outset. Chapters begin with a writing activity that asks students to write a response to a visual. *Seeing and Writing: Skills Check* at the end of each chapter help students to revise and edit their initial Seeing and Writing response and to apply the skills they learned and practiced in the chapter.

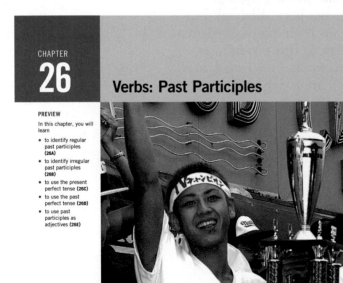

CHAPTER
26

Verbs: Past Participles

PREVIEW
In this chapter, you will learn

- to identify regular past participles **(26A)**
- to identify irregular past participles **(26B)**
- to use the present perfect tense **(26C)**
- to use the past perfect tense **(26D)**
- to use past participles as adjectives **(26E)**

WORD POWER
crave: to have a strong desire for something
envision: to imagine
anticipate: to look forward to

SEEING AND WRITING ▲
The picture above shows a winner at the Nathan's Hot Dog Eating Contest in Coney Island. Look at the picture, and then write a paragraph about something you really wanted to achieve and finally did. Explain whether you now believe the goal you achieved was worth the struggle. Try to use the Word Power words in your paragraph.

380

✓ **Seeing and Writing: Skills Check**

Look back at your response to the Seeing and Writing activity on page 380. Reread it, and complete the following tasks:

- Underline the helping verbs and past participles.
- Check to make sure that you have used these tenses correctly.
- Cross out any incorrect verb forms, and write your corrections above the line.

Then, revise and edit your paragraph.

Focus boxes. Throughout the book, Focus boxes highlight useful information, identify key points, and explain difficult concepts.

FOCUS

Writing Essay Exams

If an exam question asks you to write an essay, remember that what you are really being asked to do is to write a **thesis-and-support essay**. Chapter 14 tells you how to do this.

Numerous opportunities for practice and review. *Foundations First* helps students practice grammar in the context of exercises (many of which are connected-discourse exercises) that mirror the kinds of material they are likely to read and write both in college and in their communities.

- *Grammar in Context* **boxes in the paragraph chapters (5–13)** help students identify and correct common grammar problems related to the rhetorical pattern they are learning. Cross-references to *Foundations First*'s grammar chapters direct students to sections where they can get additional help on the grammar issues they find the most challenging.

GRAMMAR IN CONTEXT

Description

When you write a descriptive paragraph, you sometimes use **modifiers**—words and phrases that describe another word or group of words.

A modifier should be placed as close as possible to the word it is supposed to modify. If you place modifying words or phrases too far from the words they modify, you create a **misplaced modifier** that will confuse readers.

CONFUSING   Seated in a chair, the long Civil War has clearly exhausted Lincoln. (Was the Civil War seated in a chair?)

CLEAR   Seated in a chair, Lincoln is clearly exhausted by the long Civil War.

For information on how to identify and correct misplaced modifiers, see Chapter 24.

- *Self-Assessment Checklists* guide students as they revise and edit their work.

- *Chapter Reviews*—featuring *Editing Practices, Collaborative Activities*, and *Review Checklists*—encourage students to think critically about their writing. Finally, *Answers to Odd-Numbered Exercises* at the end of the book enable students to check their own work as they practice and review.

- *Unit Reviews* **that allow students to practice editing in realistic situations.** New end-of-unit essays contain multiple types of errors, allowing students to identify and correct the errors they are likely to encounter in their own writing. More practice is available online in **extra Unit Reviews** in the *Exercise Central* **database,** the largest online collection of grammar and writing exercises.

A strong visual appeal for basic writing students. More than two-dozen visual writing prompts help students generate ideas for writing. Thumbnail photos in the Editing Practices provide cultural contexts as well as support for students who are visual learners. In addition, the easy-to-navigate, full-color design engages students and helps them locate information quickly and easily.

An emphasis on the connection between reading and writing. *Foundations First* presents reading as an integral part of the writing process, offering numerous student and professional examples throughout the text. Chapter 2, "Reading Strategies," introduces the basic techniques of active reading and shows students how to get the most out of their academic and professional reading. Seventeen selections (three of them by students) in Chapter 37, "Readings for Writers," provide material for writing assignments and classroom discussion.

An integrated approach to building vocabulary. In every chapter, *Word Power* boxes introduce new words and encourage students to use them in the context of their own writing. Appendix A, "Building Word Power," gives students additional opportunities for expanding their vocabulary.

Extensive help for ESL students. Chapter 30 addresses the concerns of nonnative writers. *ESL Tips* throughout the *Instructor's Annotated Edition* provide helpful hints for novice and experienced instructors alike.

Practical help with college and workplace skills. Chapter 1, "Practical Strategies," gives students insight into skills, such as note-taking and time management, that they will need to succeed in college, while Appendix B, "Strategies for Workplace Success," discusses important real-world skills such as writing résumés and cover letters and preparing for job interviews.

Content that respects students as serious writers. The tone and level of the discussions and examples as well as the subject matter of the exercises acknowledge the diverse interests, ages, and experiences of developmental students.

New to This Edition

We have worked hard to make the fourth edition of *Foundations First* even more useful to developmental writers and their instructors. Based on suggestions from our users, we streamlined the instructions, examples, exercises, and marginal notes to make the text simpler, cleaner, and more accessible to basic writing students. Additionally, we added chapters that cover basic study skills and other issues that help students make a successful transition to college.

More support for success in college

- **New College Communication Skills section in Chapter 1, "Practical Strategies,"** helps students interact more successfully with other students and with their instructors, whether in class, in person, or by email. Coverage includes advice on clarity; tone; and what to avoid in emails to instructors.

- **New Strategies for College Success tips** in every chapter reinforce the advice presented in Chapter 1 and help students adjust to the academic environment. Tips focus on everything from understanding the limits of spell checkers to taking good notes in class.

STRATEGIES FOR COLLEGE SUCCESS

Proofreading Your Work

After running a spell check, proofread your work to catch typos such as *if* for *is* or *mush* for *much*. For additional tips on how to become a successful student, see Chapter 1.

- **A new annotated student essay in Chapter 14, "Writing an Essay,"** about the pros and cons of using Facebook, gives students more help with basics like topic sentences, thesis statements, and support in their writing.

New readings and student essays. Chapter 37, "Readings for Writers," includes seventeen selections chosen for their currency and interest. Nine of these essays are new, including selections by Henry Louis Gates Jr., Maxine Hong Kingston, and professional skateboarder Tony Hawk.

Thoroughly revised and updated exercises that engage student interest. Abundant new exercises throughout the book cover diverse subjects in the areas of work, academics, historical events, cultural issues, and everyday life. New exercise topics include manga; Supreme Court Justice Sonia Sotomayer; blogs and social networking sites; the Nobel Peace Prize; locally grown food; and animal experimentation.

Online and Print Resources for Students

Foundations First does not stop with the book. Online and in print, you will find both free and affordable premium resources to help students get even more out of the book and your course. We also offer convenient instructor resources, such as diagnostic and mastery tests, classroom activities, transparency masters, and more. To order any of the products below, or to learn more about them, contact your Bedford/St. Martin's sales representative by emailing Sales Support at sales_support@bfwpub.com, or visit the Web site at **bedfordstmartins.com/foundationsfirst/catalog.**

Companion Web site for *Foundations First* at bedfordstmartins.com/ foundationsfirst Send students to free and open resources, or upgrade to an expanding collection of innovative digital content—all in one place. The companion Web site provides access to *Exercise Central*, the largest free online database of editing exercises and annotated model student paragraphs and essays. Premium resources available through the companion Web site for *Foundations First* or packaged with the text include *WritingClass* and *Re:Writing Plus*.

- *WritingClass* **at yourwritingclass.com** *WritingClass* makes it easy for you to set assignments—and see when students have done them. At one easy-to-use site, students can see if there is a new assignment, do the work, and check back to find out how they did. New pre-built modules let you quickly assign a targeted series of activities on a single topic. There are options for building online discussions, adding multimedia tutorials, and more—but you choose how much or how little you want to do online.

- *Re:Writing Plus,* **now with** *VideoCentral,* **at bedfordstmartins .com/rewritingbasics** This impressive resource gathers all of our premium digital content for the writing class into one online collection. It includes innovative and interactive help with writing a paragraph; tutorials and practices that show how writing works in students' real-world experience; *VideoCentral,* with over fifty brief videos for the writing classroom; the first-ever peer review game; *i•cite: visualizing sources;* plus hundreds of models of writing and hundreds of readings. *Re:Writing Plus* can be purchased separately or packaged with *Foundations First* at a significant discount.

Exercise Central 3.0 **at bedfordstmartins.com/exercisecentral** Completely free, *Exercise Central 3.0* is the largest database of editing exercises on the Internet and a comprehensive resource for skill development as well as skill assessment. In addition to providing over 9,000 exercises offering immediate feedback and reporting to an instructor grade book, *Exercise Central 3.0* can help identify students' strengths and weaknesses, recommend personalized study plans, and provide tutorials for common problems.

Supplemental Exercises for Foundations First, **Fourth Edition (ISBN: 978-0-312-58371-2)** This print ancillary provides students with even more practice on essential skills and can be packaged at a discount.

Exercise Central to Go: Writing and Grammar Practices for Basic Writers **CD-ROM (ISBN: 978-0-312-58961-5)** provides hundreds of practice items to help students build their writing and editing skills. No Internet connection necessary.

Make-a-Paragraph Kit with Exercise Central to Go **(ISBN: 978-0-312-58966-0)** This fun, interactive CD-ROM includes "Extreme Paragraph Makeover," a brief animation teaching students about paragraph development. It also contains exercises to help students build their own paragraphs, audiovisual tutorials on four of the most common errors for basic writers, and the content from *Exercise Central to Go: Writing and Grammar Practices for Basic Writers.*

The Bedford/St. Martin's ESL Workbook, **Second Edition (ISBN: 978-0-312-54034-0)** This comprehensive collection of exercises covers grammatical issues for multilingual students with varying English-language skills and cultural backgrounds. Instructional introductions precede exercises in a broad range of topic areas.

The Bedford/St. Martin's Planner **(ISBN: 978-0-312-57447-9)** This appealing resource includes everything that students need to plan and use their time effectively, with advice on preparing schedules and to-do lists, and with blank schedules and calendars (monthly and weekly) for planning. Integrated into the planner are pointers on fixing common grammar errors, advice on note taking and succeeding on tests, an address book, and an annotated list of useful Web sites.

Journal Writing: A Beginning **(ISBN: 978-0-312-58923-3)** Designed to give students an opportunity to use writing as a way to explore their thoughts and feelings, this writing journal includes a generous supply of inspirational quotations placed throughout the pages, tips for journaling, and suggested journal topics.

From Practice to Mastery **(for the Florida College Basic Skills Exit Tests) (ISBN: 978-0-312-69268-1)** Full of practical instruction and plenty of examples, this handy book gives students all the resources they need to practice for and pass the Florida College Basic Skills Exit Tests on reading and writing.

For Instructors

Instructor's Annotated Edition of *Foundations First,* **Fourth Edition (ISBN: 978-0-312-60318-2)** Contains answers to all of the practice exercises, plus numerous ESL and teaching tips that offer ideas, reminders, and cross-references that are immediately helpful to teachers at any level.

Classroom Resources for Instructors Using Foundations First, **Fourth Edition (ISBN: 978-0-312-58368-2)** Offers advice for teaching developmental writing as well as chapter-by-chapter pointers for using *Foundations First* in the classroom. It contains answers to all of the book's practice exercises, sample syllabi, additional teaching materials, and full chapters on collaborative learning.

Diagnostic and Mastery Tests for Foundations First, **Fourth Edition (ISBN: 978-0-312-58369-9)** Offers diagnostic and mastery tests that complement the topics covered in *Foundations First.*

Transparency Masters for Foundations First, **Fourth Edition (ISBN: 978-0-312-58373-6)** Includes numerous models of student writing and is downloadable from the *Foundations First* Web site at **bedfordstmartins .com/foundationsfirst.**

Testing Tool Kit: A Writing and Grammar Test Bank (ISBN: 978-0-312-43032-0)   This test bank CD-ROM allows instructors to create secure, customized tests and quizzes from a pool of nearly 2,000 questions covering forty-seven topics. It also includes ten pre-built diagnostic tests.

Teaching Developmental Writing: Background Readings, Third Edition (ISBN: 978-0-312-43283-6)   Edited by Susan Naomi Bernstein, this professional resource is a print volume offering a collection of essays on topics of interest to basic writing instructors, along with editorial apparatus pointing out practical classroom applications. This edition includes revised chapters on technology and the writing process and focuses on topics relevant to instructors who work with multilingual students in the developmental writing course.

The Bedford Bibliography for Teachers of Basic Writing, Third Edition (ISBN: 978-0-312-58154-1) **(also available online at bedfordstmartins .com/basicbib)**   Compiled by members of the Conference on Basic Writing under the general editorship of Gregory R. Glau and Chitralekha Duttagupta, this annotated list of books, articles, and periodicals was created specifically to help teachers of basic writing find valuable resources.

TeachingCentral at bedfordstmartins.com/teachingcentral   Offers the entire list of Bedford/St. Martin's print and online professional resources in one place. You will find landmark reference works, sourcebooks on pedagogical issues, award-winning collections, and practical advice for the classroom—all free for instructors.

Content cartridges   These are available for the most common course management systems—Blackboard, WebCT, Angel, and Desire2Learn—and allow you to easily download Bedford/St. Martin's digital materials for your course. For more information about our course management offerings, visit **bedfordstmartins.com/cms**.

CourseSmart e-Book for Foundations First (ISBN: 978-0-312-60359-5)   We have partnered with CourseSmart to offer a downloadable or online version of *Foundations First*, Fourth Edition, at about half the price of the print book. To learn more about this low-cost alternative visit **www .coursesmart.com**.

Ordering Information

Use these ISBNs to order the following supplements packaged with your students' books:
Foundations First, **Fourth Edition, with:**

- *The Bedford/St. Martin's ESL Workbook*, Second Edition
  ISBN: 978-0-312-58960-8

- *The Bedford/St. Martin's Planner*
  ISBN: 978-0-312-58965-3

- *Exercise Central to Go* CD-ROM
  ISBN: 978-0-312-58961-5

- *From Practice to Mastery* (for Florida)
  ISBN: 978-0-312-69268-1
- *Journal Writing: A Beginning*
  ISBN: 978-0-312-58923-3
- *Make-a-Paragraph Kit* CD-ROM
  ISBN: 978-0-312-58966-0
- *Re:Writing Plus* Access Card
  ISBN: 978-0-312-58962-2
- *Supplemental Exercises*
  ISBN: 978-0-312-58371-2
- *WritingClass*
  ISBN: 978-0-312-58964-6

Acknowledgments

In our work on *Foundations First*, we have benefited from the help of a great many people.

Franklin E. Horowitz of Teachers College, Columbia University, drafted an early version of Chapter 30, "Grammar and Usage Issues for ESL Writers," and his linguist's insight continues to inform that chapter. Linda Stine of Lincoln University devoted her energy and vision to the preparation of *Classroom Resources for Instructors Using Foundations First*. Linda Mason Austin of McLennan Community College drew on her extensive experience to contribute Teaching Tips and ESL Tips to the *Instructor's Annotated Edition*. Susan Bernstein's work on the compilation and annotation of *Teaching Developmental Writing: Background Readings* reflects her deep commitment to scholarship and teaching. We are very grateful for their contributions.

We thank Kristen Blanco, Stephanie Hopkins, Judith Lechner, Carolyn Lengel, Carol Sullivan, Jessica Carroll, Charlotte Gale, Pamela Gerth, and Beth Castrodale for their contributions to the exercises and writing activities in the text, and Linda Stine for developing the PowerPoint presentation featured on the *Foundations First* Web site.

Foundations First could not exist without our students, whose words appear on almost every page of the book in sample sentences, paragraphs, and essays. We thank all of them, past and present, who have allowed us to use their work.

Instructors throughout the country have contributed suggestions and encouragement at various stages of the book's development. For their collegial support, we thank John Allison, Tomkins-Cortland Community College; Connie Baumgardner, Cleveland State Community College; Cheyenne M. Bonnell, Copper Mountain College; Lory Conrad, University of Arkansas–Fort Smith; Lisa Currie, Lord Fairfax Community College; Nissa Dalager, Rasmussen College; Beverly F. Dile, Elizabethtown Community and Technical College; Theresa Dolan, Los Angeles Trade-Technical College; William Donohue, Lincoln University; Stacey DuVal, University of Arkansas–Fort Smith; Michael Eskayo, Harold Washington Community College; Jane P. Gamber, Hutchinson Community College; Lilian Gamble, Delgado Community College; Joy Hancock, Mount San Antonio College; Stephanie Holt, Hopkinsville Community College; Debra Justice, Hopkinsville

Community College; Susan J. Kaplan, Tompkins–Cortland Community College; Lolann (Lola) King, Trinity Valley Community College; Scott H. Lowe, Hillsborough Community College; Jonah S. Macbeth, Lord Fairfax Community College; Patricia A. McDonald, Neosho Count Community College; Joshua Mattern, Waubonsee Community College; Christine Ondaro, Miami Dade College; Cheryl Reed, San Diego Miramar College; Catherine Rusco, Muskegon Community College; Jennifer Schaefer, Lord Fairfax Community College; Shusmita Sen, Spokane Community College; Denielle True, Manatee Community College; DeAnn Welch, Fort Scott Community College; and Margaret Whitley, New Mexico Junior College.

At Bedford/St. Martin's, we thank founder and former president Chuck Christensen and president Joan Feinberg, who believed in this project and gave us support and encouragement from the outset. We thank Karen Henry, editor in chief, and Erica Appel, director of development, for overseeing this edition. We are also grateful to Shannon Walsh, associate editor, and Alyssa Demirjian, editorial assistant, for helping with numerous tasks, big and small; Nancy Myers, senior production supervisor; William Imbornoni, senior project editor, for guiding the book ably through production; and Lucy Krikorian, art director, for once again overseeing a beautiful and innovative design. Thanks also go to Christina Shea, marketing manager, and her team and to our outstanding copyeditor, Rosemary Winfield, and excellent proofreader, Julie Nemer. And finally, we thank our editor, Ellen Darion, whose hard work and dedication kept the project moving along.

We are grateful, too, for the continued support of our families. Finally, we are grateful for the survival and growth of the writing partnership we entered into when we were graduate students. We had no idea then of the wonderful places our collaborative efforts would take us. Now, we know.

Laurie G. Kirszner
Stephen R. Mandell

Contents

UNIT ONE

Learning Strategies for College Success   1

1   Practical Strategies   3

UNIT FOUR

Solving Common Sentence Problems 289

20 Run-Ons 291

21 Sentence Fragments 306

UNIT FIVE

Understanding Basic Grammar 365

UNIT SIX

Understanding Punctuation, Mechanics, and Spelling 479

A

Appendix A: Building Word Power 601

B

Appendix B: Strategies for Workplace Success 609

A Note to Students

It's no secret that writing will be very important in most of the courses you take in college. Whether you write lab reports or English papers, midterms or final exams, your ability to organize your thoughts and express them in writing will help to determine how well you do. In other words, succeeding at writing is the first step toward succeeding in college. Perhaps even more important, writing is a key to success outside the classroom. On the job and in everyday life, if you can express yourself clearly and effectively, you will stand a better chance of achieving your goals and making a difference in the world.

Whether you write as a student, as an employee, as a parent, or as a concerned citizen, your writing almost always has a specific purpose. For example, when you write an essay, a memo, a letter, or a research paper, you are writing not just to complete an exercise but to give other people information or to tell them your ideas or opinions. That is why, in this book, we don't just ask you to do grammar exercises and fill in blanks; in each chapter, we also ask you to apply the skills you are learning to a writing assignment of your own.

As teachers—and as former students—we know how demanding college can be and how hard it is to juggle assignments with work and family responsibilities. We also know that you don't want to waste your time. That's why in *Foundations First* we make information easy to find and use and include many different features to help you become a better writer.

Laurie G. Kirszner
Stephen R. Mandell

Strategies for College Success

Strategies for College Success tips throughout the book give you more help adjusting to the academic world, taking the general advice presented in Chapter 1 and applying it in the context of specific activities and assignments.

Self-Assessment Checklists for Revising and Editing Your Writing

Unit Two of *Foundations First* includes a series of Self-Assessment Checklists to help you write, revise, and edit paragraphs and essays. You can use these checklists in your writing course and in other courses that include written assignments. The page number for each checklist is included here.

Foundations First
Sentences and Paragraphs

WITH READINGS

UNIT ONE

Learning Strategies for College Success

Practical Strategies

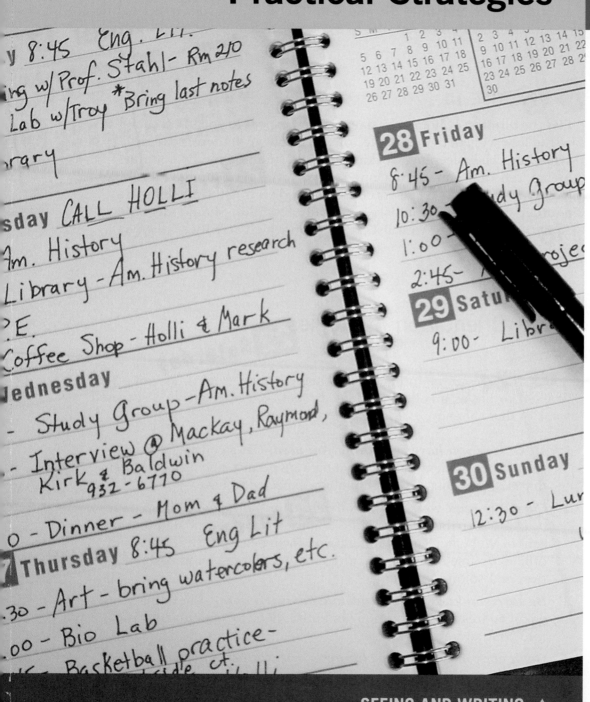

Handwritten organizer entries:

y 8:45   Eng. Lit.
ng w/ Prof. Stahl - Rm 210
Lab w/Troy *Bring last notes
rary

sday CALL HOLLI

Am. History
Library - Am. History research
.E.
Coffee Shop - Holli & Mark

ednesday
- Study Group - Am. History
- Interview @ Mackay, Raymond,
  Kirk & Baldwin
        932-6770
0 - Dinner - Mom & Dad
Thursday 8:45   Eng Lit
.30 - Art - bring watercolors, etc.
.00 - Bio Lab
Basketball practice-

28 Friday
8:45 - Am. History
10:30 - ...dy Group
1:00 - ...
2:45 - ...
29 Satu...
9:00 - Libr...

30 Sunday
12:30 - Lu...

PREVIEW

In this chapter, you will learn

- orientation strategies (**1A**)
- first-week strategies (**1B**)
- day-to-day strategies (**1C**)
- note-taking strategies (**1D**)
- homework strategies (**1E**)
- exam-taking strategies (**1F**)
- time-management strategies (**1G**)
- college communication skills (**1H**)
- Internet strategies (**1I**)

SEEING AND WRITING ▲

The picture above shows two pages of a busy student's organizer. How do you manage to fit everything you need to do into the limited time you have? Look at the picture, and then write a few sentences that answer this question. Try to use the Word Power word in your response.

WORD POWER

prioritize: to deal with tasks in order of importance

By deciding to go to college, you have decided to make some important changes in your life. In the long run, you will find that the changes will be positive, but there will be some challenges as well. One way in which your life will change is that now, perhaps more than ever, you will find yourself short of time. Life will become a balancing act as you juggle classroom time, commuting time, work time, and study time along with family responsibilities and time for yourself. The strategies discussed in this chapter can help make your life as a college student more productive and less stressful.

▌ PRACTICE 1-1 ▐

List the number of hours per day that you expect to spend on each of the following activities while you are a college student: reading, attending class, sleeping, working at a job, fulfilling family commitments, relaxing, commuting, and studying. (Be sure you have a total of twenty-four hours.) When you have finished your list, trade lists with another student, and compare your daily activities. Should any other activities be added to your list? If so, from which activities will you subtract time?

A Orientation Strategies

Some strategies come in handy even before school begins, as you orient yourself to life as a college student. In fact, you've probably discovered some of them already.

1. *Make sure you have everything you need.* Get a college catalog, a photo ID, a student handbook, a parking permit, and any other items that new students at your school are expected to have.

2. *Carefully read your school's orientation materials.* These materials are distributed as handouts and perhaps also posted on the school Web site. They will help you locate campus buildings and offices, course offerings, faculty members, extracurricular activities, and so on.

3. *Be sure you know your academic advisor's name.* Check his or her email address, office location, and office hours. Copy this information into your address book.

4. *Get a copy of your college library's orientation materials.* These will tell you about the library's hours and services and explain procedures such as how to use the online catalog.

5. *Be sure you know where things are.* You need to know how to find the library and the parking lot and also where you can do photocopying or buy a newspaper.

Home Page of Hillsborough Community College Web Site

■ PRACTICE 1-2

Visit your school's Web site. List the three most useful pieces of information you find there. Now, compare your list with those of other students in your class. Did reading their lists lead you to reevaluate your own? Do you still think the three items you listed are the most useful?

1. _____

2. _____

3. _____

■ PRACTICE 1-3

Working in a group of three or four students, draw a rough map of your school's campus. Include the general locations of the library, the financial aid office, the registrar's office, the cashier, the cafeteria, the bookstore, the computer lab, the campus police, and the student health office. Now, make up a quiz for another group of students, asking them to locate three additional buildings or offices on their map.

B First-Week Strategies

College can seem like a confusing place at first, but from your first day as a college student, there are steps you can take to help you get your bearings.

1. *Make yourself at home.* Find places on campus where you can get something to eat or drink, and find a good place to study or relax before or between classes. As you explore the campus, try to locate all the things you may need — for example, ATMs and restrooms.

2. *Know where you're going and when you need to be there.* Check the building and room number for each of your classes and the days and hours the class meets. Copy this information onto the front cover of the appropriate notebook. Pay particular attention to classes with irregular schedules (for example, a class that meets from 9 a.m. to 10 a.m. on Tuesdays but from 11 a.m. to 12 noon on Thursdays).

3. *Introduce yourself to other students.* Networking with other students is an important part of the college experience. Get the name, phone number, and email address of two students in each of your classes. If you miss class, you will need to get in touch with someone to find out what material you missed.

4. *Familiarize yourself with each course's syllabus.* At the first meeting of every course, your instructor will hand out a syllabus. (The syllabus may also be posted on the course's Web page.) A syllabus gives you three kinds of useful information:

   - Information that can help you plan a study schedule — for example, when assignments are due and when exams are scheduled
   - Practical information, such as the instructor's office number and email address and the books and supplies you need to buy
   - Information about the instructor's policies on absences, grading, class participation, and so on

5. *Buy books and supplies with care.* When you buy your books and supplies, be sure to keep the receipts, and don't write your name in your books until you are certain that you are not going to drop a course. (If you write in a book, you will not be able to return it for a full refund.) If your roster of courses is not definite, you should wait a few days to buy your texts. You should, however, buy some items right away — for example, a separate notebook and folder for each course you are taking and a college dictionary. In addition to the books and other items required for a particular course (for example, a lab notebook, a programmable calculator, and art supplies), you should buy pens and pencils in different colors as well as paper clips or a stapler, Post-it notes, highlighter pens, and so on — and a backpack or bookbag in which to keep all these items.

WORD POWER

networking: interacting with others to share information

WORD POWER

syllabus: an outline or summary of a course's main points (the plural form is *syllabi*)

For information about how to use an organizer, see **1G**.

FOCUS

Using a Dictionary

Even though your word-processing program will have a spell checker, you still need to buy a dictionary. A college dictionary tells you not only how to spell words but also what words mean and how to use them. (For more on using a dictionary, see Appendix A.)

---

6. **Set up your notebooks.** Establish a separate notebook (or a separate section of a divided notebook) for each of your classes. (Notebooks with pocket folders can help you keep graded papers, worksheets, handouts, and other important documents all in one place.) Copy your instructor's name, email address, phone number, and office hours and location onto the inside front cover of the notebook. Write your own name and email address or phone number on the outside, along with the class schedule.

■ PRACTICE 1-4

Set up a notebook for each course you are taking. Then, exchange notebooks with another student, and review each other's notebooks.

C Day-to-Day Strategies

As you get busier and busier, you may find it hard to keep everything under control. Here are some strategies to help you as you move through the semester.

1. **Find a place to study.** As a college student, you will need your own private place to work and study. Even if it's just a desk in one corner of your dorm room (or, if you are living at home or off campus, in one corner of your bedroom), you will need a place that is yours alone — a place that will be undisturbed when you leave it. (The kitchen table, which you share with roommates or family members, will not work.) This space should include everything you will need to make your work easier — quiet, good lighting, a comfortable chair, a clean work surface, storage for supplies, and so on.

2. **Set up a bookshelf.** Keep your textbooks, dictionary, calculator, supplies, and everything else you use regularly for your coursework in one place — ideally, in your own workspace. That way, when you need something, you will know exactly where it is.

3. **Set up a study schedule.** Identify thirty- to forty-five-minute blocks of free time before, between, and after classes. Set this time aside for review. Remember, studying should be part of your regular routine, not something you do only the night before an exam.

WORD POWER

priorities: things considered more important than others

4. ***Establish priorities.*** It's important to understand what your priorities are. The first step in establishing priorities is to find out which assignments are due first, which ones can be done in steps, and which tasks or steps will be most time consuming. Then, you must decide which tasks are most pressing. (For example, studying for a test to be given the next day is more pressing than reviewing notes for a test scheduled for the following week.) Finally, you have to decide which tasks are more important than others. For example, studying for a midterm is more important than studying for a quiz, and the midterm for a course you are in danger of failing is more important than the midterm for a course in which you are doing well. Remember, you can't do everything at once; you need to decide what must be done immediately and what can wait.

5. ***Check your mail.*** Check your campus email regularly — if possible, several times a day. If you miss a message, you may miss important information about changes in assignments, canceled classes, or rescheduled quizzes.

6. ***Schedule conferences.*** Try to meet with each of your instructors during the semester even if you are not required to do so. You might schedule one conference during the second or third week of school and another a week or two before a major exam or paper is due. These meetings will help you understand exactly what is expected of you, and your instructors will appreciate and respect your initiative.

7. ***Become familiar with the student services available on your campus.*** College is hard work, and you can't do everything on your own. There is nothing wrong with getting help from your school's writing center or tutoring center or from the center for students with disabilities (which serves students with learning disabilities as well as physical challenges), the office of international students, or the counseling center, as well as from your adviser or course instructors.

Asking for Help

Despite all your careful planning, you may still run into trouble. For example, you may miss an exam and have to make it up; you may miss several days of classes in a row and fall behind in your work; you may have trouble understanding the material in one of your courses; or a family member may get sick. Don't wait until you are overwhelmed to ask for help. If you have an ongoing personal problem or a family emergency, let your instructors know immediately.

PRACTICE 1-5

Try to figure out how and when you study best. Do you do your best studying in the morning or late at night? Alone or in a busy library? When you know the answers to these questions, set up a weekly study schedule. Begin by identifying your free time and deciding how you can use it most efficiently. Next, discuss your schedule with a group of three or four other students. How much time does each of you have available? How much time do you think you need? Does the group consider each student's study schedule to be realistic? If not, why not?

D Note-Taking Strategies

Learning to take notes in a college class takes practice, but taking good notes is essential for success in college. Here are some basic guidelines that will help you develop and improve your note-taking skills.

During Class

1. *Come to class.* If you miss class, you miss notes — so come to class, and come on time. In class, sit where you can see the board and hear the instructor. Don't feel you have to keep sitting in the same place in each class every day; change your seat until you find a spot that's comfortable for you.

2. *Date your notes.* Begin each class by writing the date at the top of the page. Instructors frequently identify material that will be on a test by dates. If you do not date your notes, you may not know what to study.

3. *Know what to write down.* You can't write down everything an instructor says. Listen carefully *before* you write, and listen for cues to what's important. For example, sometimes the instructor will tell you that something is important or that a particular piece of information will be on a test. Sometimes he or she will write key terms and concepts on the board. If the instructor emphasizes an idea or

Student Reviewing Notes

underlines it on the board, you should do the same in your notes. (Of course, if you have done the assigned reading before class, you will recognize important topics and know to take especially careful notes when these topics are introduced in class.)

4. *Include examples.* Try to write down an example for each general concept introduced in class — something that will help you remember what the instructor was talking about. (If you don't have time to include examples as you take notes during class, add them when you review your notes.) For instance, if your world history instructor is explaining *nationalism*, you should write down not only a definition but also an example, such as "Germany in 1848."

5. *Write legibly, and use helpful signals.* Use dark (blue or black) ink for your note-taking, but keep a red or green pen handy to highlight important information, jot down announcements (such as a change in a test date), note gaps in your notes, or question confusing points. Do not take notes in pencil, which is hard to read and less permanent than ink.

6. *Ask questions.* If you do not hear (or do not understand) something your instructor says, or if you need an example to help you understand something, *ask!* But don't immediately turn to another student for clarification. Instead, wait to see if the instructor explains further or if he or she pauses to ask if anyone has a question. If you're not comfortable asking a question during class, make a note of the question and ask the instructor — or send an email — after class.

After Class

1. ***Review your notes.*** After every class, try to spend ten or fifteen minutes rereading your notes, filling in gaps and adding examples while the material is still fresh in your mind. When you review, try giving each day's notes a title so you can remember the topic of each class. This will help you locate information when you study.

2. ***Recopy information.*** When you have a break between classes or when you get home, recopy important pieces of information from your notes:

    *   Copy announcements (such as quiz dates) onto your calendar.
    *   Copy reminders (for example, a note to schedule a conference before your next paper is due) into your organizer.
    *   Write questions you want to ask the instructor onto the top of the next blank page in your notes.

Before the Next Class

1. ***Reread your notes.*** Leave time just before each class to skim the previous class's notes once more. This strategy will get you oriented for the class to come and remind you of anything that needs clarification or further explanation.

2. ***Ask for help.*** Call or email a classmate if you need to fill in missing information. If you still need help, see the instructor during office hours, or come to class early to ask your question before class begins.

■ PRACTICE 1-6 ■

Compare the notes you took in one of your classes with notes taken by another student in the same class. How are your notes different? Do you think you need to make any changes in the way you take notes?

E Homework Strategies

Doing homework is an important part of learning in college. Homework gives you a chance to practice your skills and measure your progress. If you are having trouble with the homework, chances are you are having trouble with the course. Ask the instructor or teaching assistant for help *now*; don't wait until the day before the exam. Here are some tips for getting the most out of your homework.

1. ***Write down the assignment.*** Don't expect to remember an assignment; copy it down. If you are not sure exactly what you are supposed to do, check with your instructor or with another student.

2. ***Do your homework, and do it on time.*** Teachers assign homework to reinforce classwork, and they expect homework to be done on a regular basis. It is easy to fall behind in college, and trying to do three — or five — nights' worth of homework in one night is not a good idea. If you do several assignments at once, you not only overload yourself but also miss important day-to-day connections with classwork.

3. ***Be an active reader.*** Get into the habit of highlighting your textbooks and other material as you read. (For specific strategies for active reading, see Chapter 2.)

4. ***Join study groups.*** A study group of three or four students can be a valuable support system for homework as well as for exams. If your schedule permits, do some homework assignments — or at least review your homework — with other students on a regular basis. In addition to learning information, you will learn different strategies for doing assignments.

■ PRACTICE 1-7

Working in a group of three or four students, list the ways in which a study group might benefit you. How many students should be in the group? How often should they meet? Should the group include students whose study habits are similar or different? What kind of help do you think you would need? What kind of help could you offer to other students?

F Exam-Taking Strategies

Preparation for an exam should begin well before the exam is announced. In a sense, you begin this preparation on the first day of class.

Exam Book

Before the Exam

1. *Attend every class.* Regular attendance in class — where you can listen, ask questions, and take notes — is the best possible preparation for exams. If you do have to miss a class, arrange to copy (and read) another student's notes *before the next class* so you will be able to follow the discussion.

2. *Keep up with the reading.* Read every assignment, and read it before the class in which it will be discussed. If you don't, you may have trouble understanding what is going on in class.

3. *Take careful notes.* Take careful, thorough notes, but be selective. If you can, compare your notes on a regular basis with those of one or two other students in the class; working together, you can fill in gaps or correct errors. Establishing a buddy system will also force you to review your notes regularly instead of just on the night before the exam.

4. *Study on your own.* When an exam is announced, adjust your study schedule — and your priorities — so you have time to review everything. (This is especially important if you have more than one exam in a short period of time.) Review all your material (class notes, readings, and so on), and then review it again. Make a note of anything you don't understand, and keep track of topics you need to review. Try to predict the most likely questions and — if you have time — practice answering them.

5. *Study with a group.* If you can, set up a study group. Studying with others can help you understand the material better. However, don't come to group sessions unprepared and expect to get all the information you need from the other students. You must first study on your own.

6. *Make an appointment with your instructor.* Make an appointment with the instructor or with the course's teaching assistant a few days before the exam. Bring to this conference any specific questions you have about course content and about the format of the upcoming exam. (Be sure to review all your study material before the conference.)

7. *Review the material one last time.* The night before the exam is not the time to begin studying; it is the time to review. When you have finished your review, get a good night's sleep.

During the Exam

Like an athlete before a big game or a musician before an important concert, you will already have done all you could to get ready for the test by the time you walk into the exam room. Your goal now is to keep the momentum going and not do anything to undermine all your hard work.

WORD POWER

undermine: to weaken support for something

1. *Read through the entire exam.* Be sure you understand how much time you have, how many points each question is worth, and exactly what each question is asking you to do. Many exam questions call for just a short answer — *yes* or *no, true* or *false.* Others ask you to

fill in a blank with a few words, and still others require you to select the best answer from among several choices. If you are not certain what kind of answer a particular question calls for, ask the instructor or the proctor *before* you begin to write. (Remember, on some tests there is no penalty for guessing, but on other tests it is best to answer only those questions you have time to read and consider carefully.)

FOCUS

Writing Essay Exams

If an exam question asks you to write an essay, remember that what you are really being asked to do is to write a **thesis-and-support essay**. Chapter 14 tells you how to do this.

---

2. ***Budget your time.*** Once you understand how much each section of the exam and each question are worth, plan your time and set your priorities, devoting the most time to the most important questions. If you know you tend to rush through exams, or if you find you often run out of time before you get to the end of a test, you might try putting a mark on your paper when about one-third of the allotted time has passed (for a one-hour exam, put a mark on your paper after twenty minutes) to make sure you are pacing yourself appropriately.

3. ***Reread each question.*** Carefully reread each question before you start to answer it. Underline the **key words** — the words that give specific information about how to approach the question and how to phrase your answer.

FOCUS

Key Words

Here are some helpful key words to look for in exam questions.

analyze	explain	suggest results, effects, outcomes
argue	give examples	
compare	identify	summarize
contrast	illustrate	support
dcfine	recount	take a stand
demonstrate	suggest causes, ori-	trace
describe	gins, contributing	
evaluate	factors	

Remember, even if everything you write is correct, your response is not acceptable if you don't answer the question. If a question asks you to *compare* two novels, *summarizing* just one of them will not be acceptable.

4. *Brainstorm to help yourself recall the material.* If you are writing a paragraph or an essay, look frequently at the question as you **brainstorm**. (You can write your brainstorming notes on the inside cover of the exam book.) Quickly write down all the relevant points you can think of — the textbook's points, your instructor's comments, and so on. The more you can think of now, the more you will have to choose from when you write your answer. (For more on brainstorming, see 3C.)

5. *Write down the main idea.* Looking closely at the way the question is worded and at your brainstorming notes, write a sentence that states the main idea of your answer. If you are writing a paragraph, this sentence will be your **topic sentence**; if you are writing an essay, it will be your **thesis statement**.

6. *List your key points.* You don't want to waste your limited (and valuable) time writing a detailed outline, but an informal outline that lists just your key points is worth the little time it takes. An informal outline will help you plan a clear direction for your paragraph or essay.

7. *Draft your answer.* You will spend most of your time actually writing the answers to the questions on the exam. Follow your outline, keep track of time, and consult your brainstorming notes when you need to — but stay focused on your writing.

8. *Reread, revise, and edit.* When you have finished drafting your answer, reread it carefully to make sure that it says everything you want it to say — and that it answers the question.

FOCUS

Academic Honesty

Academic honesty — the standard for truth and fairness in work and behavior — is very important in college. Understanding academic honesty goes beyond simply knowing that it is dishonest to cheat on a test. To be sure you are conforming to the rules of academic honesty, follow these guidelines:

- Don't re-use papers you wrote in high school. The written work you are assigned in college is designed to help you learn, and your instructors expect you to do the work for the course when it is assigned.
- Don't copy information from a book or article or paste material from a Web site directly into your papers. Using someone else's words or ideas without proper acknowledgment constitutes **plagiarism**, a very serious offense.
- Don't ask another student (or your parents) to help you write or revise a paper. If you need help, ask your instructor or a writing center tutor.
- Don't allow another student to copy your work on a test.
- Don't allow another student to turn in a paper you wrote (or one you helped him or her write).
- Don't work with other students on a take-home exam unless your instructor gives you permission to do so.
- Never buy a paper. Even if you edit it, it is still not your own work.

WORD POWER

consistently: regularly,
steadily

G Time-Management Strategies

Learning to manage your time is important for success in college. Here are some strategies you can adopt to make this task easier.

1. **Use an organizer.** Whether you prefer to use a print organizer or the calendar or notes application on phone or laptop, you should certainly use one — and use it consistently. If you are most comfortable with paper and pencil, purchase a "week-on-two-pages" academic year organizer (one that begins in September, not January). The "week-on-two-pages" format (see p. 17) has two advantages: it gives you more writing room for Monday through Friday than for the weekend, and it also lets you view an entire week at once.

   Carry your organizer with you at all times. At the beginning of the semester, copy down key pieces of information from each course syllabus — for example, the date of every quiz and exam and the due date of every paper. As the semester progresses, continue to write in assignments and deadlines, and also enter information such as days when a class will be canceled or will meet in the computer lab or in the library, reminders to bring a particular book or piece of equipment to class, and appointments with instructors or other college personnel. If you like, you can also jot down reminders and schedule appointments that are not related to school — for example, changes in your work hours, a dentist appointment, or lunch with a friend. (In addition to writing notes on the pages for each date, some students like to keep a separate month-by-month "to do" list. Crossing out completed items can give you a feeling of accomplishment — and make the road ahead look shorter.)

   On the following page, the first sample organizer pages show how you can use an organizer to keep track of deadlines, appointments, and reminders. The second sample organizer pages include not only this information but also a study schedule, with notes about particular tasks to be done each day.

2. **Use a calendar.** Buy a large calendar, and post it where you will see it every morning — for example, on your desk, on the refrigerator, or wherever you keep your keys and your student ID. At the beginning of the semester, fill in important dates such as school holidays, work commitments, exam dates, and due dates for papers and projects. When you return from class each day, update the calendar with any new information you have entered into your organizer.

3. **Plan ahead.** If you think you will need help from a writing-center tutor to revise a paper that is due in two weeks, don't wait until day thirteen to try to make an appointment; all the time slots may be filled by then. To be safe, make an appointment for help about a week in advance.

4. **Learn to enjoy downtime.** One final — and important — point to remember is that you are entitled to "waste" a little time. When you have a free minute, take time for yourself — and don't feel guilty about it.

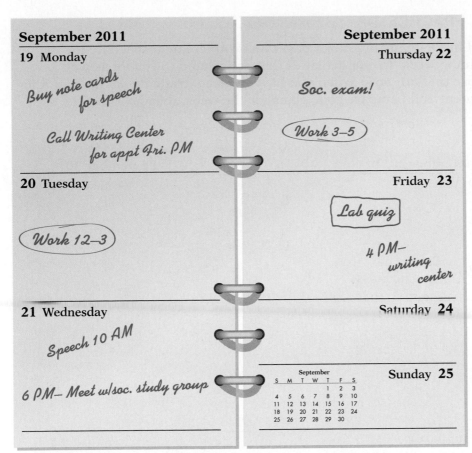

September 2011

19 Monday

*Buy note cards
for speech*

*Call Writing Center
for appt Fri. PM*

20 Tuesday

Work 12–3

21 Wednesday

Speech 10 AM

6 PM– Meet w/soc. study group

September 2011

Thursday 22

Soc. exam!

Work 3–5

Friday 23

Lab quiz

*4 PM–
writing
center*

Saturday 24

September						
S	M	T	W	T	F	S
				1	2	3
4	5	6	7	8	9	10
11	12	13	14	15	16	17
18	19	20	21	22	23	24
25	26	27	28	29	30	

Sunday 25

Sample Organizer Pages: Deadlines, Appointments, and Reminders Only

September 2011

19 Monday

Buy note cards for speech
English paper–first draft
Call Writing Center for appt Fri. PM

20 Tuesday

Work 12–3

Recopy speech on note cards

21 Wednesday

9:30–10 Practice speech
Speech 10 AM

6 PM– Meet w/soc. study group

September 2011

Thursday 22

*AM–Reread
soc. notes*

Soc. exam!

Work 3–5

Friday 23

1–2 Review for quiz

Lab quiz

*4 PM–
writing
center*

Saturday 24

Sunday 25

September						
S	M	T	W	T	F	S
				1	2	3
4	5	6	7	8	9	10
11	12	13	14	15	16	17
18	19	20	21	22	23	24
25	26	27	28	29	30	

Sample Organizer Pages: Deadlines, Appointments, Reminders, and Study Schedule

■ **PRACTICE 1-8** ■

Fill in the blank organizer pages below to create a schedule for the
coming week. (Enter activities that are related to school as well as
those that are not.) When you have finished, trade books with another
student and compare your plans for the week ahead.

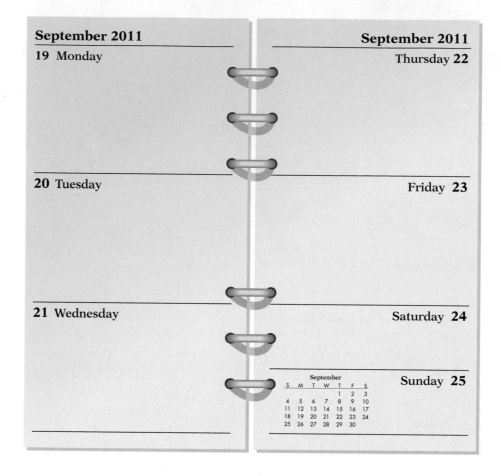

| H | # College Communications Skills |

Effective communication — both oral and written — is essential in college. Your success in college depends to a great extent on how effectively
you communicate your ideas in speech and in writing — to your instructors and to your fellow students.

Written Communication

WORD POWER

diction: choice of words;
style of expression

Your college writing should have a level of **diction** that is somewhere
between formal and informal English. You should sound conversational
but should not generally use slang, abbreviations, incorrect grammar, or
other nonstandard forms. When the situation calls for it, use the technical
vocabulary of the subject you are writing about. Choose your words carefully, and make sure you say exactly what you intend to say.

Remember that good writing is not overly complex, pompous, or flowery. Your purpose is not to impress your readers with your vocabulary but to use language that is appropriate for the occasion. For this reason, try not to use words like *utilize* when you mean *use* or *terminate* when you mean *end*.

Also be careful to avoid **offensive language** (language that is sexist or racist or that includes profanity). Sexist language intentionally (or unintentionally) degrades or excludes a gender. In your writing, always refer to adult females as *women*, not *girls* or *ladies*. In addition, do not use *he* or *him* when your subject could be either male or female. Instead, use the plural *they* or *them* or the phrase *he or she* (not *he/she*). Whenever possible, use a nonsexist alternative to a sexist usage — for example, *people* instead of *mankind* or *letter carrier* instead of *mailman*.

Electronic Communication

Most of us think of electronic communication as informal, so we use an informal style in our emails. Even though personal emails and text messages may be informal (disregarding the rules of grammar, punctuation, and spelling), the more formal emails you send to your instructors should follow the rules of standard written English.

Although the following usages are aceptable in informal electronic communication, they are *never acceptable* in academic essays or in emails to instructors:

- **Shorthand,** such as *4* for *for*, *r* for *are*, *u* for *you*, and *c* for *see*
- **Abbreviations,** such as *JK* ("just kidding"), *btw* ("by the way"), *GTG* ("got to go"), *BWTM* ("but wait, there's more"), and *TTYL* ("talk to you later")
- **Emoticons,** typed characters, such as : -) or : - (, which indicate a writer's mood or feelings
- **Inappropriate salutations,** such as *Hi Prof* or *Hey*.

Oral Communication

In general, the same advice that applies to written communication also applies to speaking. In one-on-one situations, take cues from your instructor about the level of formality that is required. Remember, it's fine to be friendly, but you need to be respectful and not overly familiar. For example, do not call a professor by his or her first name unless you are asked to do so.

When you ask a question in class, let the instructor know that you have read the assignment. For example, introduce your question with a phrase such as "According to the textbook" or "As the article you assigned says." Never begin a question with "I haven't read the assignment, but . . ."

When you speak in class, be respectful of your fellow students: listen to what they have to say, and don't interrupt. When it's your turn to speak, choose your words carefully, speak slowly, and try to make your points clearly. Use the technical language of a discipline when it is appropriate to do so. For example, use terms like *protagonist* (not *hero*), *titration* (not *mixture*), and *cohort* (not *group*) in literature, chemistry, and sociology, respectively.

As you do in written communication, use language that is suitable for the situation. Do not use slang or nonstandard constructions, and never use offensive language.

◼ PRACTICE 1-9

Write a text message to a friend in which you provide information about when and where your study group will be meeting and what you plan to do at the meeting. (Remember, you are limited to 140 characters.) Then, rewrite the text as an informal email to a friend, editing out any shorthand or abbreviations. Finally, rewrite the message as an email to your professor.

When you have finished, compare the three messages. How are they alike? How are they different?

Internet Strategies

When people refer to the Internet, they usually mean the **World Wide Web**. The Web relies on **links** — highlighted words and phrases. By clicking on these links, you can move easily from one part of a document to another or from one **Web site** (collection of documents) to another.

Finding Information on the Internet

To use the Internet, you need an Internet **browser**, a tool that enables your computer to access and display Web pages. The most popular browsers are Internet Explorer, Firefox, and Safari. (Most new computers come with one of these browsers already installed.)

Once you are online, you need to connect to a **search engine**, a program that helps you find information by searching through the millions of documents that are available on the Internet. Among the most popular search engines are Google (the most widely used) and Yahoo! A Google home page appears on the facing page.

You can use a search engine to help you access information:

- *You can enter a Web site's URL.* All search engines have a URL search box in which you can enter a Web site's **URL** (electronic address). When you hit your computer's Enter key, the search engine connects you to the Web site.

- *You can do a keyword search.* All search engines let you do a **keyword** search: you type a term (or terms) into a keyword search box, and the search engine retrieves documents that contain the term.

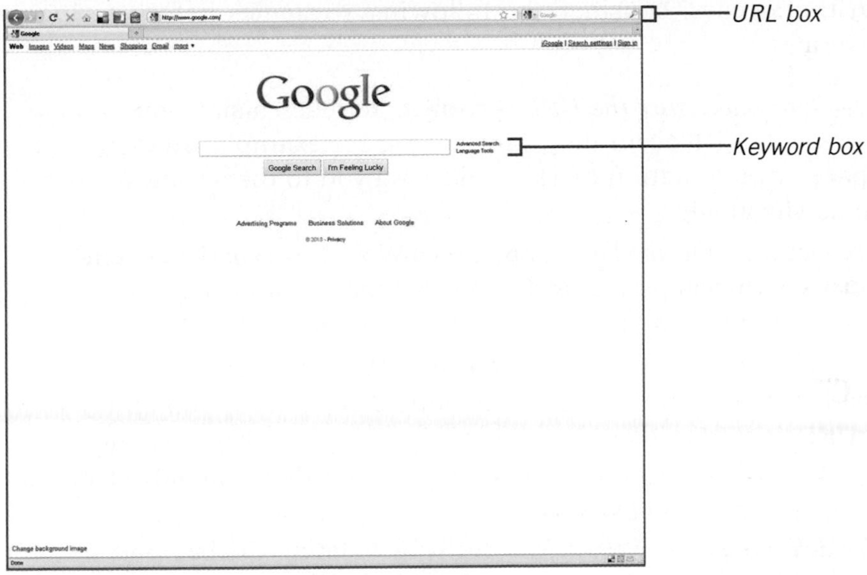

— URL box
— Keyword box

Google Home Page

- *You can do a subject search.* Some search engines, such as Yahoo!, let you do a **subject search**. First, you choose a broad subject from a list of subjects: *Computers & Internet, News & Media, Business & Economy,* and so on. Each of these general subjects leads you to more specific subjects, until eventually you get to the subtopic that you want. The Yahoo! search directory appears below.

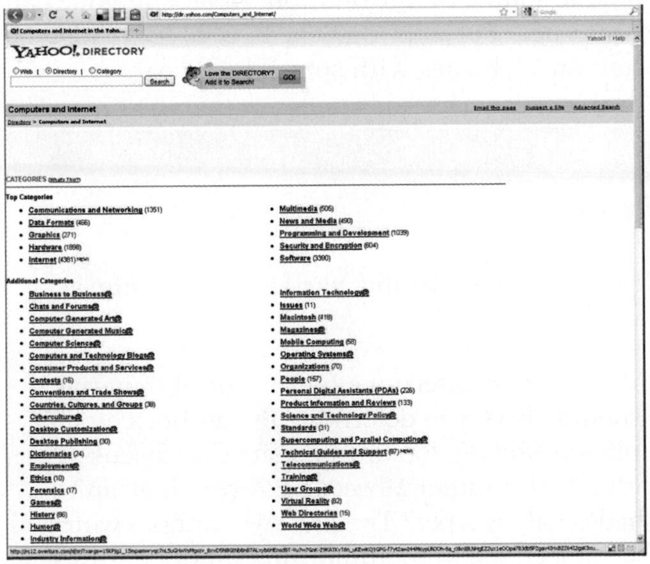

Yahoo! Search Directory

Accessing Web Sites: Troubleshooting

Sometimes you will be unable to access a site you want to visit. When this occurs, consider the following strategies before giving up:

- *Check to make sure the URL is correct.* To reach a site, you have to type its URL accurately. Any error — for example, an extra space or punctuation mark — will send you to the wrong site (or to no site at all).

- *Try revisiting the site later.* Sometimes Web sites experience temporary technical problems that prevent them from being accessed. Your computer will tell you if a site is temporarily unreachable.

- *Check to make sure the site still exists.* Web sites, especially those maintained by individuals, frequently disappear. If you entered a URL correctly, your computer is functioning properly, and you still cannot access a site after several attempts, chances are that the site no longer exists.

- *Try deleting parts of the URL.* Begin by deleting the last part of the URL — everything after the last slash. Then, try accessing the site again. If this doesn't work, delete everything up to the next slash. As a last resort, try to reach the site's home page — the first part of the URL. Once you get to the home page, follow the links to the part of the Web site that you want.

Evaluating Web Sites

Not every Web site is a valuable source of information. In fact, anyone can post information on the Internet. For this reason, it is a good idea to approach the content posted on Web sites with some skepticism.

Evaluating Web Sites

To decide whether to use information from a particular Web site, ask the following questions:

- *Is the site reliable?* Always try to determine the author of material on a Web site. You should also try to determine the author's qualifications. For example, say you are looking at a site that discusses Labrador retrievers. Is the author a breeder? A veterinarian? Someone who has had a Lab as a pet? The first two authors would be authorities on the subject; the third author might not be.

- *Does the site have a hidden purpose?* When you evaluate a Web site, be sure to consider its purpose. For example, a site discussing

(continued on following page)

Evaluating Web Sites, *continued from previous page*

the health benefits of herbal medicine would have one purpose if it were sponsored by a university and another purpose if it were sponsored by a company selling herbal remedies.

- *Is the site up-to-date?* If a site has not been recently updated, you should carefully consider the information it contains. A discussion of swine flu in the United States, for example, would be out of date if it were written before the widespread outbreak in 2009 and 2010. You would have to continue your search until you found a more current discussion.

- *Is the information on the site trustworthy?* A site should include evidence — facts and expert opinion — to support what it says. If it does not contain such evidence, you should consider the information to be just someone's unsupported personal opinion.

You can get a general sense of a Web site's purpose (and about its intended audience) by looking at the last part of its URL. Here are some of the common endings.

.com stands for *commercial*. If you see this at the end of a URL, you can be reasonably sure that the site was created to sell something.

.org stands for *organization*. If you see this at the end of a URL, you can be reasonably sure that the site was created by a nonprofit organization — for example, a charitable or religious group.

.edu stands for *education*. If you see this at the end of a URL, you can be reasonably sure that the site was created by an educational institution.

.gov stands for *government*. If you see this at the end of a URL, you can be reasonably sure that the site was created by a government agency.

Using the Internet to Locate Information

You can use the Internet to find information about the subjects you are studying. Certain sites, such as the following ones, can help you access information related to your courses.

Art History

Art History on the Web
   witcombe.sbc.edu
   /ARTHLinks.html

Education

Education World
  education-world.com

Literature

On-Line Books Page
  digital.library.upenn
  .edu/books

Science

Scirus
  scirus.com

Sociology

Social Sciences
  davidcoon.com/soc.htm

You can also use the Internet for help with your writing. Below are just a few of the many Web sites that you can consult to answer questions that may come up as you write.

Advice on Revision

Paradigm Online Writing Assistant
english.ttu.edu/kairos/3.1/news
/paradigm/revision.htm

Tips on Grammar

The Online English Grammar
edunet.com/English
/grammar

Help in Writing Paragraphs

Purposes of Paragraphs
owl.english.purdue.edu/owl
/resource/606/01

Tips on Proofreading

Tips for Effective Proofreading
unc.edu/depts/wcweb
/handouts/proofanswer.html

Finally, you can use the Internet to locate everyday information. For example, you can access news and weather reports, download voter registration information, get directions, obtain consumer information, or even apply for a job. The following sites are just a few of the many resources available on the Internet.

Dictionaries

yourDictionary.com
yourdictionary.com

Maps and Directions

MapBlast!
mapblast.com

Employment

America's Job Bank
jobbankinfo.org

Newspapers

Newspapers.com
newspapers.com

Law and Legal Information

American Law Sources Online
lawsource.com/also

Telephone Directories

Switchboard.com
switchboard.com

FOCUS

Web Sites

For a comprehensive list of useful Web sites, go to the *Foundations First* Web site: bedfordstmartins.com/foundationsfirst.

■ PRACTICE 1-10

At home or in your school's computer lab, practice entering five of the URLs listed on pages 23–24. Make sure you enter the URLs exactly as they appear on the page. If entering a URL does not take you to the appropriate Web site, check to make sure that you entered the URL correctly. (If the site is no longer active, choose another URL from the list.)

PRACTICE 1-11

Working in a group of four students, select one of the Web sites listed on pages 23–24. At home or in your school's computer lab, access the site and make a list of three things you like and three things you dislike about it. Then, exchange lists with another student in your group. On what do you agree? On what do you disagree?

PRACTICE 1-12

Use a search engine to locate a Web site that focuses on a topic you know a lot about — for example, your hometown, a famous person, or a sport. Evaluate the site according to the guidelines listed on pages 22–23.

 Seeing and Writing: Skills Check

Look back at your response to the Seeing and Writing activity on page 3. Now that you have read the information in this chapter, you should have a better idea of how to manage your time in the weeks and months to come:

- How do you think you will fit everything into your schedule?
- Which of the strategies described in this chapter do you think you will find most helpful?

Expand your Seeing and Writing response so that it answers these questions. Then, revise and edit your work.

✓ **Review Checklist**

Strategies for College Success

- ☐ Some strategies come in handy even before school begins. (See 1A.)

- ☐ From your first day as a college student, there are steps you can take to help you get your bearings. (See 1B.)

- ☐ Day-to-day strategies can help you move through the semester. (See 1C.)

- ☐ Learning to take good notes is essential for success in college. (See 1D.)

- ☐ Doing homework gives you a chance to practice your skills and measure your progress. (See 1E.)

- ☐ Preparation for an exam should begin well before the exam is announced. (See 1F.)

(continued on following page)

Review Checklist, *continued from previous page*

☐ Learning to manage your time is important for success in college. (See 1G.)

☐ Knowing what kind of language to use in academic situations is an important skill for college students. (See 1H.)

☐ Knowing how to use the Internet can help you succeed in college and beyond. (See 1I.)

Reading Strategies

Why are frogs croaking?

Amphibians—frogs, toads, and salamanders—have been around for a long time. They watched the dinosaurs come and go. But today amphibian populations around the world are in dramatic decline, with more than a third of the world's amphibian species threatened with extinction. Why?

Biologists work to answer this question by making observations and doing experiments. A number of factors may be involved, and one possible cause may be the effects of agricultural pesticides and herbicides. Several studies have shown that many of these chemicals tested at realistic concentrations do not kill amphibians. But Tyrone Hayes, a biologist at the University of California at Berkeley, probed deeper.

Hayes focused on atrazine, the most widely used herbicide in the world and a common contaminant in fresh water. More than 70 million pounds of atrazine are applied to farmland in the United States every year, and it is used in at least 20 countries. Atrazine is usually applied in the spring, when many amphibians are breeding and thousands of tadpoles swim in the ditches, ponds, and streams that receive runoff from farms.

In his laboratory, Hayes and his associates raised frog tadpoles in water containing no atrazine and in water with concentrations ranging from 0.01 parts per billion (ppb) up to 25 ppb. The U.S. Environmental Protection Agency considers environmental levels of atrazine of 10 to 20 ppb of no concern; the level it considers safe in drinking water is 3 ppb. Rainwater in Iowa has been measured to contain 40 ppb. In Switzerland, where the use of atrazine is illegal, the chemical has been measured at approximately 1 ppb in rainwater.

In the Hayes laboratory, concentrations as low as 0.1 ppb had a dramatic effect on tadpole development: it feminized the males. In some of the adult males that developed from these larvae, the vocal structures used in mating calls were smaller than normal, female sex organs developed, and eggs were found growing in the testes. In other studies, normal adult male frogs exposed to 25 ppb had a tenfold reduction in testosterone levels and did not produce sperm. You can imagine the disastrous effects these developmental and hormonal changes could have on the capacity of frogs to breed and reproduce.

But Hayes's experiments were performed in the laboratory, with a species of frog bred for laboratory use. Would his results be the same in nature? To find out, he and his students traveled from Utah to Iowa, sampling water and collecting frogs. They analyzed the water

Frogs Are Having Serious Problems An alarming number of species of frogs, such as this tiny leaf frog (*Agalychnis calcarifer*) from Ecuador, are in danger of becoming extinct. The numerous possible reasons for the decline in global amphibian populations have been a subject of widespread scientific investigation.

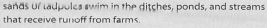

SEEING AND WRITING ▲

The picture above shows a page of a textbook with important information highlighted and notes in the margins. When you read your textbooks, you will understand them better if you write notes directly on the pages. Write a few sentences explaining how you mark your textbooks — or explaining why you don't. Try to use the Word Power words in your response.

PREVIEW

In this chapter, you will learn

- how to become an active reader **(2A)**

- how to preview, highlight, annotate, outline, and summarize a reading assignment **(2B)**

- how to read different kinds of texts **(2C)**

WORD POWER

highlight: to mark a page to emphasize important details

annotate: to make explanatory notes on a page

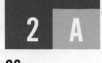

A   Becoming an Active Reader

Reading is essential in all your college courses. To get the most out of your college reading, you should be prepared to take a critical stance— commenting on, questioning, evaluating, and even challenging what you read. In other words, you should learn to become an active reader.

In practical terms, being an **active reader** means actively participating in the reading process—approaching a reading assignment with a clear understanding of your purpose and writing in the text to help you understand what you are reading.

You may find it easier to understand the concept of active reading if you see how this strategy applies to "reading" a picture. Like a written text, every **visual text**—a photograph, an advertisement, a chart, or a graph; a work of fine art, such as a painting or a piece of sculpture; and even a Web site—has a message to communicate. Visual texts communicate their messages through the specific words and images they choose and through the way these words and images are arranged on the page.

When you approach a visual, your first step is to identify the words and images you see. Then, you consider how they are arranged and how they are related to one another.

In the following ad for Tropicana orange juice, the main idea—that the product's juicier pulp gives it a fresh-squeezed taste—is expressed in the heading: "We squeeze the oranges, not the pulp." This message is supported by the large central image, which links the juice carton, the glass of juice, and the orange. The smaller type presents specific information that explains how and why this brand of juice is fresher and tastier than others.

Tropicana Advertisement

Questions for Tropicana Ad (p. 28)

- ☐ Why is the orange labeled "Handle with Care"?

- ☐ Why is it placed in front of the juice carton?

- ☐ Does this ad convince consumers to purchase Tropicana rather than another brand?

- ☐ If so, why? If not, why not?

In the visual below, a painting by the American artist Winslow Homer, the images are not supported by written text, but the message is still clear. Here, the central image—the man alone in the middle of the ocean, surrounded by open space—communicates the painting's emotions: fear, desperation, hopelessness. The surrounding images—the choppy waves, the threatening sky, the sharks—support this impression.

Winslow Homer, The Gulf Stream (1899)

The Metropolitan Museum of Art, Catharine Lorillard Wolfe Collection, Wolfe Fund, 1906. (06.1234) Photograph (c) 1995, The Metropolitan Museum of Art

When you "read" visuals such as these, at first you get just a general sense of what you see. But as you read more actively, you let your mind take you beyond the page. You ask yourself why certain details were selected, why they are arranged as they are, what comes to mind when you see the picture, and whether you find the visual effective.

Questions for Winslow Homer Painting (p. 29)

☐ What is the man looking at?

☐ Does he see anything in the distance?

☐ Why is he alone on the ocean?

☐ Is the painting frightening?

☐ Would it be different if the artist had used lighter colors?

☐ Would it be different if the artist had added or deleted any details?

Active reading of a written text, like active reading of a visual text, is a writing activity that encourages you to "read between the lines." In this way, it helps you develop a deeper understanding of the material. The process of actively reading a written text is explained and illustrated in the following section.

B Reading Written Texts

Determining Your Purpose

Even before you start reading, you should consider some questions about your **purpose**—why you are reading. The answers to these questions will help you understand what kind of information you hope to get out of your reading and how you will use this information.

Questions about Your Purpose

☐ Will you be expected to discuss what you are reading? If so, will you discuss it in class? In a conference with your instructor?

☐ Will you have to write about what you are reading? If so, will you be expected to write an informal response (for example, a journal entry) or a more formal one (for example, an essay)?

☐ Will you be tested on the material?

Previewing

When you **preview**, you try to get a sense of the writer's main idea, key supporting points, and general emphasis. You can begin by focusing on the title, the first paragraph (which often contains a purpose statement or overview), and the last paragraph (which often contains a summary of the writer's points). You should also look for clues to the writer's message in the passage's **visual signals** and **verbal signals**.

Using Visual Signals

☐ Look at the title.

☐ Look at the opening and closing paragraphs.

☐ Look at each paragraph's first sentence.

☐ Look at headings.

☐ Look at *italicized* and **boldfaced** words.

☐ Look at numbered lists.

☐ Look at bulleted lists (like this one).

☐ Look at visuals (graphs, charts, tables, photographs, and so on).

☐ Look at any information that is boxed.

☐ Look at any information that is in color.

Using Verbal Signals

☐ Look for phrases that signal emphasis ("The *primary* reason"; "The *most important* idea").

☐ Look for repeated words and phrases.

☐ Look for words that signal addition (*also, in addition, furthermore*).

☐ Look for words that signal time sequence (*first, after, then, next, finally*).

☐ Look for words that identify causes and effects (*because, as a result, for this reason*).

☐ Look for words that introduce examples (*for example, for instance*).

☐ Look for words that signal comparison (*likewise, similarly*).

☐ Look for words that signal contrast (*unlike, although, in contrast*).

☐ Look for words that signal contradiction (*however, on the contrary*).

☐ Look for words that signal a narrowing of the writer's focus (*in fact, specifically, in other words*).

☐ Look for words that signal summaries or conclusions (*to sum up, in conclusion*).

When you have finished previewing, you should have a general sense of what the writer wants to communicate.

■ PRACTICE 2-1 ■

Following is a brief newspaper article by Nathan Black, a Colorado high
school student. Preview the article in preparation for class discussion as
well as for the other activities that will be assigned throughout section 2B.

As you read, try to identify the writer's main idea and key supporting points, and write that information on the blank lines that follow
the article.

After a Shooting

Nathan Black

High school students in Littleton now have a new excuse to get out of class   1
for a few extra minutes: the lockdown drill. My school had its first last year.
While most students sat quietly in locked classrooms, a few teachers responded
to simulated crises, like a student injury. It's one of many new features of life in
Littleton since the Columbine High shootings of 1999. Most people have tried to
move on, but some aspects of our lives have changed forever.

That reality will soon face the people of Santee, California, where two students   2
were killed on Monday. And the shooting yesterday of a girl by a schoolmate in
Pennsylvania and the arrest this week of two boys in Twentynine Palms, California,
after police found a "hit list" of their classmates, suggest that Columbine's
experience will become still more common.

Apart from lockdown drills, there have been few changes in security procedures.   3
The greatest change has been the increase of paranoia. For example, a few weeks
after the shooting I was working on a graph assignment with a friend. We arranged
the points on the graph to spell out a humorous but inappropriate message.

A month earlier, my friend would have said, "The teacher's going to be mad."   4
This time he said, "If we turn this in, we'll be expelled."

There's the difference. The worst case I've heard of took place in Canada. A   5
boy had written and performed, for class, a dark, vengeful monologue. After his
performance, rumors swirled about hit lists, and the boy was arrested. The police
said he had made death threats. No hard evidence appears to have been found in
the boy's home — just the monologue. His story has now entered the larger tale of
Littleton and its aftermath.

Only time can ease this paranoia. I wish time would hurry up about it.   6

Yet good changes have also occurred. The killings at Columbine and elsewhere   7
have been a pitiless wake-up call to adults. Last April, 1,500 of my peers gathered
at a local college to discuss education. Adults want our perspective. They may
want it now because of fear, but they want it.

Such conversations have to continue. Violence is still happening, and as long   8
as my school needs a lockdown drill, we need to keep asking: Why do kids kill
each other, and how can we stop them? There's no answer yet. But the fact that
we're looking makes me feel a little less helpless.

Main idea

_____

_____

Key supporting points

1. _____

   _____

2. _____

   _____

3. _____

   _____

4. _____

   _____

Highlighting

After you have previewed a passage, read it again, this time more carefully.
As you read, keep a pen (or a highlighter pen) handy so you can **highlight**,
using underlining and symbols to identify important information. This
active reading strategy will reinforce your understanding of the writer's
main idea and key supporting points and will help you see the relationships among them. (If you want to highlight material in a book that you
do not own, photocopy the passage.)

Highlighting Symbols

☐ <u>Underline</u> or ▢highlight▢ key ideas.

☐ ▢Box▢ or ⬭circle⬭ words or phrases you want to remember.

☐ Place a check mark (✓) or star (✱) next to an important idea.

☐ Place a double check mark (✓✓) or double star (✱✱) next to an especially significant idea.

☐ Draw lines or arrows to connect related ideas.

☐ Put a question mark beside a word or idea that you do not understand.

☐ Number the writer's key supporting points or examples.

Highlight freely, but try not to highlight too much. Remember, you will eventually have to read every highlighted word, phrase, and sentence—and your study time is limited. Highlight only the most important, most useful information—for example, definitions, examples, and summaries.

FOCUS

Knowing What to Highlight

You want to highlight what's important—but how do you *know* what's important?

▪ Look for the same **visual signals** you looked for when you did your previewing. Many of the ideas you will need to highlight will probably be found in material that is visually set off from the rest of the text—opening and closing paragraphs, lists, and so on.

▪ Look for **verbal signals**—words and phrases like *however, therefore, another reason,* and *the most important point*—that often introduce key points.

Together, these visual and verbal signals will give you clues to the writer's meaning and emphasis.

Here is how a student highlighted a passage from an introductory American history textbook. The passage focuses on the position of African Americans in society in the years immediately following World War II. Because the passage includes no visual signals apart from the title and paragraph divisions, the student looked carefully for verbal signals to guide her highlighting.

"I spent four years in the army to free a bunch of Frenchmen and

Dutchmen," an African-American corporal declared, "and I'm hanged

if I'm going to let the Alabama version of the Germans kick me around

✓ when I get home." Black veterans as well as civilians resolved that the

return to peace would not be a return to the racial injustices of prewar
America. Their political (clout) had grown with the migration of two million African Americans to northern and western cities, where they could vote and their ballots could make a difference. Even in the South, the proportion of blacks who could vote inched up from 2 percent to 12 percent in the 1940s. Pursuing civil rights through the courts and Congress, the National Association for the Advancement of Colored People (NAACP) counted half a million members.

In the postwar years, individual African Americans broke through the color barrier, achieving several ("firsts.") Jackie Robinson integrated major league baseball when he played for the Brooklyn Dodgers in 1947, braving abuse from fans and players to win the Rookie of the Year Award. In 1950, Ralph J. Bunche received the Nobel Peace Prize for his United Nations work, and Gwendolyn Brooks was awarded the Pulitzer Prize for poetry. Charlie "Bird" Parker, Ella Fitzgerald, and a host of other black musicians were hugely popular across racial lines.

Still, for most African Americans, little had changed, especially in the South, where violence greeted their attempts to assert their rights. Armed ① white men turned back Medgar Evers (who would become a key civil rights leader in the 1960s) and four other veterans trying to vote in Mississippi. A mob lynched Isaac Nixon for voting in Georgia, and an all-white ② jury acquitted the men accused of his murder. In the South, governors, U.S. senators, other politicians, and local vigilantes routinely intimidated ③ potential black voters with threats of economic retaliation and violence.

> — James L. Roark et al., *The American Promise*, Fourth Edition

The student who highlighted this passage was preparing for a meeting of her study group. Because the class would be taking a midterm the following week, she needed to understand the material.

The student began her highlighting by placing check marks beside two important advances for African Americans cited in paragraph 1 and by drawing arrows to specific examples of blacks' political influence. (Although she thought she knew the meaning of the word *clout*, she circled it anyway and placed a question mark above it to remind herself to check its meaning in a dictionary.)

In paragraph 2, she boxed the names of prominent postwar African Americans and underlined their contributions, circling and starring the key word "firsts." She then underlined and double-starred the entire passage's main idea—the first sentence of paragraph 3—numbering the examples in the paragraph that support this idea.

■ PRACTICE 2-2

Review the highlighted passage from the history textbook (pp. 34–35). How would your own highlighting of this passage be similar to or different from the sample student highlighting?

■ PRACTICE 2-3

Reread "After a Shooting" (pp. 32–33). As you read, highlight the passage by underlining and starring main ideas, boxing and circling key words, and checkmarking important points. Circle each unfamiliar word, and put a question mark above it.

Annotating

As you highlight, you should also annotate what you are reading. **Annotating** a passage means reading critically and making notes—of questions, reactions, reminders, and ideas for discussion or writing—in the margins or between the lines. Keeping a record of ideas as they occur to you will help prepare you to discuss the reading with your classmates—and, eventually, to write about it.

Considering the following questions as you read will help you read critically and write useful annotations.

Questions for Critical Reading

☐ What is the writer saying?

☐ What is the writer's purpose—his or her reason for writing?

☐ What kind of audience is the writer addressing?

☐ Is the writer responding to another writer's ideas?

☐ What is the writer's main idea?

☐ How does the writer support his or her points? With facts? Opinions? Both facts and opinions? What supporting details and examples does the writer use?

☐ Does the writer include enough supporting details and examples?

☐ Do you understand the writer's vocabulary?

☐ Do you understand the writer's ideas?

☐ Do you agree with the points the writer is making?

☐ Do you see any connections between this reading assignment and something else you have read?

The following passage reproduces the student's highlighting of the American history textbook from pages 34–35 and also illustrates her annotations.

"I spent four years in the army to free a bunch of Frenchmen and Dutchmen," an African-American corporal declared, "and I'm hanged if I'm going to let the Alabama version of the Germans kick me around when ✓ I get home." Black veterans as well as civilians resolved that the return to peace would not be a return to the racial injustices of prewar America. ✓ Their political (clout) had grown with the migration of two million Afri- can Americans to northern and western cities, where they could vote and their ballots could make a difference. Even in the South, the proportion of blacks who could vote inched up from 2 percent to 12 percent in the 1940s. Pursuing civil rights through the courts and Congress, the National Association for the Advancement of Colored People (NAACP) counted half a million members.

(?) = power

In the postwar years, individual African Americans broke through the color barrier, achieving several "firsts." Jackie Robinson integrated major league baseball when he played first base for the Brooklyn Dodgers in 1947, braving abuse from fans and players to win the Rookie of the Year Award. In 1950, Ralph J. Bunche received the Nobel Peace Prize for his United Nations work, and Gwendolyn Brooks was awarded the Pulitzer Prize for poetry. Charlie "Bird" Parker, Ella Fitzgerald, and a host of other black musicians were hugely popular across racial lines.

✱ ✱ Still, for most African Americans, little had changed, especially in the South, where violence greeted their attempts to assert their rights. Armed white men turned back Medgar Evers (who would become a key ① civil rights leader in the 1960s) and four other veterans trying to vote in Mississippi. A mob lynched Isaac Nixon for voting in Georgia, and ② an all-white jury acquitted the men accused of his murder. In the South, governors, U.S. senators, other politicians, and local vigilantes routinely ③ intimidated potential black voters with threats of economic retaliation and violence.

— James L. Roark et al., *The American Promise,* Fourth Edition

Margin annotations:

Achievements of African Americans:

Military

Politics

Sports

World politics

Literature

Music

In South, voters intimidated

In her annotations, this student put some of the writer's key ideas into her own words and recorded ideas she hoped to discuss in her study group.

PRACTICE 2-4

Reread "After a Shooting" (pp. 32–33). As you reread, refer to the Questions for Critical Reading (p. 36), and use them to guide you as you write your own ideas and questions in the margins. Note where you agree or disagree with the writer, and briefly explain why. Quickly summarize any points you think are particularly important. Take time to look up any unfamiliar words you have circled, and write brief definitions for them.

PRACTICE 2-5

Trade books with another student, and read over his or her highlighting and annotating of "After a Shooting." How are your written responses similar to the other student's? How are they different? Do your classmate's responses help you to see anything new about the article?

Outlining

Another technique you can use to help you understand a reading assignment better is **outlining**. Unlike a **formal outline**, which follows fairly strict conventions, an **informal outline** is easy to make and can be a valuable reading tool: it shows you which ideas are more important than others, and it shows you how ideas are related.

To make an informal outline of a reading assignment, follow these guidelines.

FOCUS

Making an Informal Outline

1. Write or type the passage's main idea at the top of a sheet of paper.
2. At the left margin, write down the most important idea of the first paragraph or section of the passage.
3. Indent the next line a few spaces, and list the examples or details that support this idea.

(continued on following page)

Making an Informal Outline, continued from previous page

4. As ideas become more specific, indent further. (Ideas that have the same degree of importance are indented the same distance from the left margin.)

5. Repeat this process with each paragraph or section of the passage.

NOTE: Your word-processing program has an outline function that automatically formats the different levels of your outline.

The student who highlighted and annotated the textbook passage on pages 37–38 made the following informal outline to help her understand its content.

Main idea: Although African Americans had achieved a lot by the end of World War II, they still faced prejudice and violence.

- African Americans as a group had made significant advances.
    Many had served in the military.
    Political influence was growing.
        More African Americans voted.
        NAACP membership increased.

- Individual African Americans had made significant advances.
    Sports: Jackie Robinson
    World politics: Ralph Bunche
    Literature: Gwendolyn Brooks
    Music: Charlie Parker and Ella Fitzgerald

- Despite these advances, much remained the same for African Americans, especially in the South.
    Blacks faced violence and even lynching if they tried to vote.
    Elected officials and vigilantes threatened potential voters.

PRACTICE 2-6

Working on your own or in a small group, make an informal outline of "After a Shooting" (pp. 32–33). Refer to your highlighting and annotations as you construct the outline. When you have finished, check to make sure your outline shows which ideas the writer is emphasizing and how those ideas are related.

Summarizing

Once you have highlighted and annotated a passage, you may want to try summarizing it. A **summary** retells, *in your own words*, what a passage is about. A summary condenses a passage, so it leaves out all but the most important ideas. A summary generally omits most details and examples, and it does not include your own ideas or opinions.

> **FOCUS**
>
> ## Writing a Summary
>
> 1. Review your outline.
> 2. Consulting your outline, restate the passage's main idea *in your own words*.
> 3. Consulting your outline, restate the passage's supporting points. Add words and phrases between sentences where necessary to connect ideas.
> 4. Reread the original passage to make sure you haven't left out anything significant.

The student who highlighted, annotated, and outlined the passage from the history textbook wrote the following summary.

> Although African Americans had achieved a lot by the end of World War II, they still faced prejudice and even violence. As a group, they had made significant advances, which included military service and increased participation in politics, as indicated by voting and NAACP membership. Individual African Americans had also made significant advances in sports, world politics, literature, and music. Despite these advances, however, much remained the same for African Americans after World War II. Their situation was especially bad in the South. For example, African Americans still faced the threat of violence and even lynching if they tried to vote. Elected officials and vigilantes also discouraged blacks from voting, often threatening them with violence.

■ PRACTICE 2-7 ■

Write a brief summary of "After a Shooting" (pp. 32–33). Use your outline as a guide, and remember to keep your summary short and to the point. (Note that your summary will be shorter than the original passage.)

C Reading in College, in the Community, and in the Workplace

In college, in your life as a citizen of a community, and in the workplace, you will read material in a variety of different formats—for example, textbooks, newspapers, Web sites, and job-related memos, letters, emails, and reports.

2   C

41
Reading in
College, in the
Community, and
in the Workplace

Although the active reading process you have just reviewed can be applied to all kinds of material, various kinds of reading often require slightly different strategies during the previewing stage. One reason for this is that different kinds of reading may have different purposes—to present information, to persuade, and so on. Another reason is that the various texts you read are aimed at different audiences, and different audiences require different signals about content and emphasis. For these reasons, you need to look for different kinds of verbal and visual signals when you preview different kinds of reading material.

Reading Textbooks

Much of the reading you do in college is in textbooks (like this one). The purpose of a textbook is to present information, and when you read a textbook, your goal is to understand that information. To do this, you need to figure out which ideas are most important as well as which points support those key ideas and which examples illustrate them.

✓ **Checklist**

Reading Textbooks

Look for the following features as you preview:

☐ **Boldfaced** and *italicized* words, which can indicate terms to be defined

☐ Boxed checklists or summaries, which may appear at the ends of sections or chapters

☐ Bulleted or numbered lists, which may list key reasons or examples or summarize important material

☐ Diagrams, charts, tables, graphs, photographs, and other visuals that illustrate the writer's points

---

■ **PRACTICE 2-8** ■

The following passage from an introductory psychology textbook defines and illustrates the term *attribution*. Identify the passage's visual and verbal signals, and use them to help you identify the main idea and key supporting points. Then, highlight and annotate the passage.

ATTRIBUTION
Explaining Behavior

Key Theme

- Attribution refers to the process of explaining your own behavior and the behavior of other people.

Key Questions

- What are the fundamental attribution error, the actor-observer discrepancy, and the self-serving bias?
- How do attributional biases affect our judgments about the causes of behavior?
- How does culture affect attributional processes?

As you're studying in the college library, the activities of two workers catch your attention. The two men are trying to lift and move a large file cabinet. "Okay, let's lift it and tip it this way," one guy says with considerable authority. In unison, they heave and tip the file cabinet. When they do, all four file drawers come flying out, bonking the first guy on the head. As the file cabinet goes crashing to the floor, you bite your lip to keep from laughing and think to yourself, "Yeah, they're obviously a pair of 40-watt bulbs."

Blaming the Victim *Fifteen-year-old Shawn Hornbeck is shown at a press conference, shortly after being reunited with his family. Four years earlier, Shawn had been kidnapped and held captive. When the FBI suspected Shawn's kidnapper in the abduction of another boy, both boys were rescued. As details of Shawn's captivity became public, many people asked why Shawn hadn't tried to escape or call the police while his kidnapper was at work. As it turned out, the kidnapper had abused and terrorized Shawn for months. At one point, he tried to strangle Shawn. When Shawn pleaded for his life, the kidnapper made the boy promise that he would never try to escape. "There wasn't a day when I didn't think that he'd just kill me," Shawn later recalled. Why do people often "blame the victim" after crimes, accidents, or other tragedies?*

Why did you arrive at that conclusion? After all, it's completely possible that the workers were not dimwits. Maybe the lock on the file drawers broke. Or maybe there was some other explanation for their mishap.

Attribution is the process of inferring the cause of someone's behavior, including your own. Psychologists also use the word *attribution* to refer to the explanation you make for a particular behavior. The attributions you make have a strong influence on your thoughts and feelings about other people.

If your attribution for the file cabinet incident was that the workers were not very bright, you demonstrated a pattern that occurs consistently in explaining the behavior of other people. *We tend to spontaneously attribute the behavior of others to internal, personal characteristics, while ignoring or underestimating the effects of external, situational factors.* This bias is so common in individualistic cultures that it's called the **fundamental attribution error** (Ross, 1977). Even though it's entirely possible that situational forces are behind another person's behavior, we tend to automatically assume

2 C

43

Reading in
College, in the
Community, and
in the Workplace

that the cause is an internal, personal characteristic (Van Boven & others, 1999; Zimbardo, 2007).

The fundamental attribution error plays a role in a common explanatory pattern called **blaming the victim**. The innocent victim of a crime, disaster, or serious illness is blamed for having somehow caused the misfortune or for not having taken steps to prevent it. For example, many people blame the poor for their dire straits, the sick for bringing on their illnesses, and battered women and rape survivors for somehow "provoking" their attackers. Hindsight makes it seem as if the victim should have been able to predict and prevent what was going to happen (Goldinger & others, 2003).

Along with the fundamental attribution error, a second bias contributes to unfairly blaming the victim of misfortune. People have a strong need to believe that the world is fair—that "we get what we deserve and deserve what we get." Social psychologist Melvin Lerner (1980) calls this the **just-world hypothesis**. Blaming the victim reflects the belief that, because the world is just, the victim must have done *something* to deserve his or her fate. Why do we have a psychological need to believe in a just world? Well, if you believe the world is unfair, then no one—including you—is safe from tragic twists of fate and chance, no matter how virtuous, careful, or conscientious you may be (Ijzerman & Van Prooijen, 2008; Thornton, 1992). Thus, believing the just-world hypothesis provides a way to psychologically defend yourself against the threatening thought, "It could just as easily have been me."

— Don H. Hockenbury and Sandra K. Hockenbury, *Psychology*, Fifth Edition

When You Can't Blame the Victim *"Blaming the victim" is one way that people reestablish their belief that the world is just. But what about situations where it is impossible to justify the victim's fate, as in the case of people who died in the terrorist attacks against the United States in September 2001? Psychologist Cheryl Kaiser and her colleagues (2004) found that when people feel sympathy for the victim, they tend to use a different strategy to restore balance to the world: they advocate revenge against those who perpetrated the injustice. As Kaiser explains, "Punishing the people who perpetrated the injustice is a form of retributive justice: Although bad things happened to good people, if the bad people are punished, they will get what they deserve, which will restore justice."*

Reading Newspapers

As a student, as an employee, and as a citizen, you read school, community, local, and national newspapers. Like textbooks, newspapers communicate information. In addition to containing relatively objective news articles, however, newspapers also contain editorials (which aim to persuade) as well as feature articles (which may be designed to entertain as well as to inform).

WORD POWER

objective: not influenced by personal emotions

✓ **Checklist**

Reading Newspapers

Look for the following features as you preview:

☐ The name of the section in which the article appears (News, Business, Lifestyle, Sports, and so on)

☐ Headlines

☐ Boldfaced headings within articles

☐ Labels like *editorial, commentary,* or *opinion,* which indicate that an article is the writer's opinion

☐ Brief biographical information at the end of an opinion piece

☐ Phrases or sentences set in boldface to emphasize key points

☐ The article's first sentence, which often answers the questions *who, what, why, where, when,* and *how*

☐ The **dateline**, which tells you the city the writer is reporting from

☐ Any related articles that appear on the same page—for example, boxed information or **sidebars**, which are short articles that provide additional background on people and places mentioned in the article

☐ Photographs

■ PRACTICE 2-9 ■

Using the checklist above as a guide, preview the following newspaper article. When you have finished, highlight and annotate the article.

The wall's 1989 fall "remains a miracle."

Berlin remembers with tears, cheers

**By Melissa Eddy
and Kirsten Grieshaber**
ASSOCIATED PRESS

BERLIN—As crowds cheered, 1,000 colorful mammoth dominoes marking the path where the Berlin Wall once stood were toppled yesterday, symbolizing both the moment 20 years ago that the wall came down and the resulting fall of communist countries in Eastern Europe.

It was the finale to a day of memorial services, speeches, and events that attracted leaders from around the world, including former Soviet President Mikhail S. Gorbachev.

Angela Merkel—Germany's first chancellor to be raised in the former communist east—and Gorbachev stood shoulder to shoulder as they crossed a former fortified border-crossing point between East and West Berlin to cheers of "Gorby! Gorby!"

"Looking back, we can see many causes that led to the peaceful revolution, but it still remains a miracle," German President Horst Koehler told the leaders of all 27 European

2 C

45

Reading in
College, in the
Community, and
in the Workplace

GERO BRELOEF / Associated Press

Giant dominoes falling in a symbolic act yesterday in front of the Brandenburg Gate, along the former path of the wall.

Union countries, Russian President Dmitry A. Medvedev, and Secretary of State Hillary Rodham Clinton.

Merkel called the events of Nov. 9, 1989, an "epic" moment in history. "It was one of the happiest moments of my life," she told the tens of thousands of people packed around the Brandenburg Gate.

In a video message screened at the main event, President Obama paid tribute to the dissidents and demonstrators who ushered in the wall's demise.

"Let us never forget Nov. 9, 1989, nor the sacrifices that made it possible," Obama said to applause and cheers.

Clinton paid tribute to Germany and other countries that shook loose communist binds.

"We remember the people of the Baltics who joined hands across their land. . . . We remember the students of Prague who propelled a dissident playwright from a jail cell to the presidency," Clinton said. "And tonight we remember the Germans, and especially the Germans in the East who stood up to say, 'No More.'"

Merkel also recalled the tragic side of Nov. 9 for Germans: the Nazis' Kristall-nacht, or Night of Broken Glass—an anti-Semitic pogrom 71 years ago. At least

91 German Jews were killed, hundreds of synagogues destroyed, and thousands of Jewish businesses vandalized and looted in the state-sanctioned riots that night in 1938.

"Both show that freedom is not self-evident," Merkel said. "Freedom must be fought for. Freedom must be defended time and again."

Uwe Kross, 65, a retiree, fought back tears as he recalled watching the 1989 drama unfold, hours after a confused announcement had come that East Germany was lifting travel restrictions.

"That night, you couldn't stop people," Kross said. "They lifted the barrier and everyone poured through. . . . Normally it was very quiet up here, but that night we could hear the footsteps of those crossing, tap, tap, tap."

Merkel, one of thousands to cross that night, recalled that "before the joy of freedom came, many people suffered."

She lauded Gorbachev, 78, with whom she shared an umbrella yesterday amid a crush of hundreds, eager for a glimpse of the man many still consider a hero for his role in pushing reform in the Soviet Union. "You made this possible," she said.

Later, Merkel also thanked Germany's neighbors to the East. She welcomed several leaders who dared to stand up for democracy, including Poland's 1980s pro-democracy leader, Lech Walesa, and Miklos Nemeth, Hungary's last prime minister before communism collapsed. The two men pushed the first domino.

Music from Bon Jovi and B e e t h o v e n recalled the joy of the border's opening, which led to German reunification less than a year later and the swift demolition, after nearly three de-cades, of most of the 96-mile wall.

Visitors placing roses into cracks in a still-existing section of the Berlin Wall at the Bernauer Strasse memorial.

CARSTEN KOALL / Getty Images

Reading Web Pages

In schools, businesses, and community settings, people turn to the Web for information. However, because many Web pages are busy and crowded, reading them can require you to work hard to distinguish important information from not-so-important material.

✓ Checklist

Reading Web Pages

Look for the following features as you preview:

- [ ] The site's URL designation (.com, .org, .gov, and so on)
- [ ] Links to other sites (underlined in blue)
- [ ] Graphics
- [ ] Color
- [ ] Headings
- [ ] Boxed material
- [ ] Placement of images and text on the page
- [ ] Type size
- [ ] Photographs

▨ PRACTICE 2-10

The following is the home page of the U.S. Environmental Protection Agency. Preview this page, looking closely at the features listed in the checklist above. What information attracts your attention? Why? Do you think this page communicates its information effectively? How could its presentation be improved?

2 C

47

Reading in
College, in the
Community, and
in the Workplace

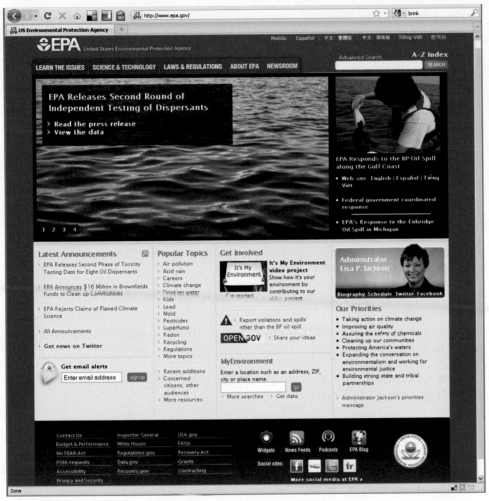

Home Page of the EPA

Reading on the Job

In your workplace, you may be called on to read memos, letters, emails, and reports. These documents are often addressed to a group rather than to a single person. (Note that the most important information is often presented *first* — in a subject line or in the first paragraph.)

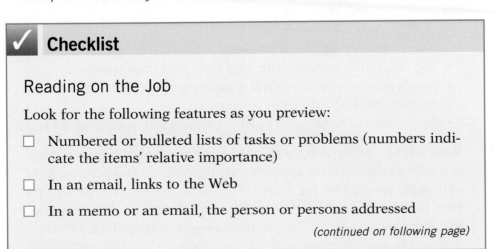

✓ **Checklist**

Reading on the Job

Look for the following features as you preview:

☐ Numbered or bulleted lists of tasks or problems (numbers indicate the items' relative importance)

☐ In an email, links to the Web

☐ In a memo or an email, the person or persons addressed

(continued on following page)

Checklist, continued from previous page

☐ In a memo or an email, the subject line

☐ In a memo or a report, headings that highlight key topics or points

☐ The first and last paragraphs and the first sentence of each body paragraph, which often contain key information

☐ Boldfaced, underlined, or italicized words

PRACTICE 2-11

Preview the following samples of on-the-job writing, and answer these questions:

- What is each writer's purpose (that is, what does the writer want to accomplish)?
- What is the most important piece of information each writer wants to communicate?

Then, highlight and annotate each sample, and write a brief summary of each in your own words.

1. A memo

September 8, 2011
To: Hector Garzon, Executive Director
From: Marco Morales, Director, Drug and Alcohol Unit
Subject: Marta Diaz-Gold

Marta Diaz-Gold has returned to work from her maternity leave. I have assigned her a caseload that consists of our clients who have been referred from the Road to Recovery program. This means that the funds for substance abuse counseling that go to Road to Recovery can now be used to pay Marta's salary and that the Road to Recovery case managers can provide support for our counseling services.

Marta and I have agreed on the following:
- Regular monthly meetings with Road to Recovery case managers
- Weekly reports to me from Marta regarding progress on the Road to Recovery caseload
- Joint review of Marta's work by Miriam Cabrera and myself after six months

Marta will be meeting with the current counselor and each individual client this week so she can make a smooth transition into her new position. As of next week, she will have full responsibility for all these clients. Because the Road to Recovery clients will not constitute a full caseload, it is understood that Marta will also be getting clients on a regular rotation from our other drug and alcohol programs.

Cc: Miriam Cabrera, Human Resources Director
    Marta Diaz-Gold

49

Reading in
College, in the
Community, and
in the Workplace

2. An email

> To: University Faculty, Staff, and Students
> Re: Emergency Closing
>
> KYW News Radio (1060) has assumed responsibility for coordinating and managing the school closing program in our area. School numbers will be announced twice every hour. The University's radio identification number is 117. The number for students attending evening classes at the University is 2117. You may also find information about school closings on the radio station's Web site at www.kyw1060.com. In addition, school closings will also be announced *by name* on WTFX-Fox TV (channel 29).

✓ Seeing and Writing: Skills Check

Look back at your response to the Seeing and Writing activity on page 27. Now that you have read this chapter, you should be able to answer the following questions:

- How do you think highlighting can help you to understand your reading assignments?
- How do you think annotating can help you to understand your reading assignments?

Expand your Seeing and Writing response so it answers these two questions. Then, revise and edit your work.

✓ Review Checklist

Reading for Academic Success

- ☐ Become an active reader. (See 2A.)
- ☐ Preview your reading assignment. (See 2B.)
- ☐ Highlight your reading assignment. (See 2B.)
- ☐ Annotate your reading assignment. (See 2B.)
- ☐ Outline your reading assignment. (See 2B.)
- ☐ Summarize your reading assignment. (See 2B.)
- ☐ Learn how to read different kinds of texts. (See 2C.)

UNIT TWO

Writing Effective Paragraphs

Writing a Paragraph

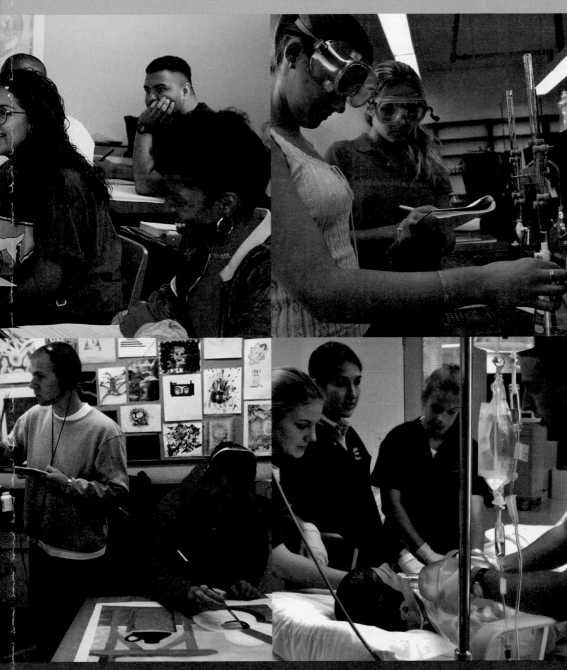

PREVIEW

In this chapter, you will learn

- to understand paragraph structure (**3A**)
- to focus on your assignment, purpose, and audience (**3B**)
- to find ideas to write about (**3C**)
- to identify your main idea and write a topic sentence (**3D**)
- to choose supporting points (**3E**)
- to arrange your supporting points (**3F**)
- to draft your paragraph (**3G**)
- to revise your paragraph (**3H**)

WORD POWER
self-esteem: pride in oneself; self-respect

SEEING AND WRITING ▲

The pictures above show college students in different settings, both traditional and nontraditional. Look at the pictures, and then consider all the reasons you decided to go to college. Think about this question carefully before you read the pages that follow. As you move through this chapter, you will be writing about the topic "Why did you decide to go to college?" Try to use the Word Power word in your response.

It's no secret that writing is essential in most of the courses you will take in college. Whether you write a lab report or an English paper, a mid-term or a final, your ability to organize your ideas and express them in writing will affect how well you do. In other words, succeeding at writing is the first step toward succeeding in college. Writing is also a key to success outside the classroom. On the job and in everyday life, if you can express yourself clearly and effectively, you will stand a better chance of achieving your goals and influencing the world around you.

This chapter will guide you through the process of writing a paragraph. Because paragraphs play an important part in almost all the writing you do, learning to write a paragraph is central to becoming an effective writer.

A Understanding Paragraph Structure

Before you can begin the process of writing a paragraph, you need to have a basic understanding of paragraph structure.

A **paragraph** is a group of sentences that is unified by a single main idea. The **topic sentence** states the main idea, and the rest of the sentences in the paragraph provide details and examples that support the main idea. At the end of the paragraph, a **concluding statement** sums up the main idea.

Paragraph Structure

Topic sentence (states main idea)

Details (support main idea)

Concluding statement (sums up main idea)

To write a paragraph, you need a main idea and convincing support. The main idea, stated in the topic sentence, unifies the paragraph. After the main idea come several sentences that support the topic sentence. These sentences present details and examples that help readers understand the paragraph's main idea. The final sentence is a concluding statement that sums up the main idea. If you follow this general structure, you are on your way to writing an effective paragraph.

Note that the first sentence of a paragraph is **indented**, starting about half an inch from the left-hand margin. Every sentence begins with a capital letter, and most end with a period. (Sometimes a sentence ends with a question mark or an exclamation point.)

B Focusing on Your Assignment, Purpose, and Audience

In college, a writing task almost always begins with an assignment. Before you begin to write, stop to ask yourself some questions about this **assignment** (*what* you are expected to write) as well as about your **purpose** (*why* you are writing) and your **audience** (*for whom* you are writing). If you answer these questions now, you will save yourself a lot of time later.

Questions about Assignment, Purpose, and Audience

Assignment

☐ What is your assignment? Is it a written assignment? Is it posted on your class Web page or syllabus?

☐ Do you have a word or page limit?

☐ When is your assignment due?

☐ Will you be expected to do your writing at home or in class?

☐ Will you be expected to work on your own or with other students?

☐ Will you be allowed to revise before (or after) you hand in your work?

Purpose

☐ Are you expected to express your personal reactions—for example, to tell how you feel about a story in the newspaper?

☐ Are you expected to present information—for example, to describe a scientific process or answer an exam question?

☐ Are you expected to take a position on a controversial issue?

Audience

☐ Who will read your paper—just your instructor or your classmates as well?

☐ Do you have an audience beyond the classroom—for example, your supervisor at work or the readers of your school newspaper?

☐ How much are your readers likely to know about your topic?

☐ Will your readers expect you to use a formal or an informal style? (For example, are you writing a research paper or a personal essay?)

■ PRACTICE 3-1

Each of the following writing tasks has a different audience and purpose. On the lines following each task, write a few notes about how you would approach the task. (The Questions about Assignment, Purpose, and Audience above can help you decide on the best approach.) When you have finished, discuss your responses with the class or in a group of three or four students.

1. For the other students in your writing class, describe the best or worst class you have ever had.

    _____

    _____

2. Write an email to your school newspaper in which you try to convince readers that a certain course should no longer be required at your school.

    _____

    _____

3. Write a letter applying for a job. Explain how the courses you have taken will help you in that job.

    _____

    _____

    _____

    _____

C Finding Ideas to Write About

Once you know what, why, and for whom you are writing, you can begin to look for ideas to write about. This process can be challenging, and it is different for every writer. You may be the kind of person who likes a structured way to find ideas, or you may prefer a looser, more relaxed way to find things to write about. As you gain more experience as a writer, you will learn which of the strategies discussed in the pages that follow work best for you.

Julia Reyes, a student in an introductory writing course, was given the following assignment.

> ASSIGNMENT Is it better to go to college right after high school or to wait? Write a paragraph in which you answer this question.

Before she could begin to draft her paragraph, Julia needed to find ideas to write about. To help students in the class practice using different ways to find ideas, Julia's instructor required them to try four different strategies—*freewriting, brainstorming, clustering,* and *journal writing.* The pages that follow explain each of these strategies and show how Julia used them.

Freewriting

When you **freewrite**, you write down whatever comes into your head, and you write for a set period of time without stopping. Grammar and spelling are not important at this point; what is important is to get your ideas down on paper. Even if your words don't seem to be going anywhere, keep on writing. Sometimes you freewrite to find a topic. Most often, however, you freewrite on a specific topic that your instructor gives you. This strategy is called **focused freewriting**.

When you finish freewriting, read what you have written, and try to find an idea you think you might be able to write more about. Underline this idea, and then freewrite again, using the underlined idea as a starting point.

Here is Julia's focused freewriting on the topic "Is it better to go to college right after high school or to wait?"

Which is better? To start college right away? To wait? I waited, but last year was such a waste of time. Such a waste. Every job I had was stupid. Telemarketing — the worst worst job. Why didn't I just quit the first day? (Money.) Waitressing was a hard job. Everybody had an attitude. The customer was always right, blah blah. Another waste of time. Why didn't I just go right to college? I needed money. And I was sick of school. School was hard. I wasn't good at it. But work was boring. But now I hate how all my friends are a year ahead of me. So I guess it's better not to wait.

Freewriting

■ PRACTICE 3-2

Read Julia's freewriting. Which ideas do you think she should write more about? Write your suggestions on the following lines.

_____

_____

_____

_____

_____

■ PRACTICE 3-3

Now, it is time for you to begin working on your own paragraph. (You already have your assignment from the Seeing and Writing box on page 53—to write about why you decided to go to college.) Your first step is to freewrite about this assignment. On a blank sheet of lined paper (or on your computer), write for at least five minutes without stopping. If you can't think of anything to write, just write the last word over and over again until something else comes to mind.

■ PRACTICE 3-4

Reread the freewriting you did for Practice 3-3. Underline the sentence that expresses the most interesting idea. Use this sentence as a starting point for another five-minute focused freewriting exercise.

Brainstorming

When you **brainstorm**, you write down all the ideas you can think of about your topic. Brainstorming is different from freewriting, and it looks different on the page. Instead of writing lines or text, you write all over the page. You can star, check, box, or underline words, and you can ask questions, make lists, and draw arrows to connect ideas.

Here are Julia's brainstorming notes on the topic "Is it better to go to college right after high school or to wait?"

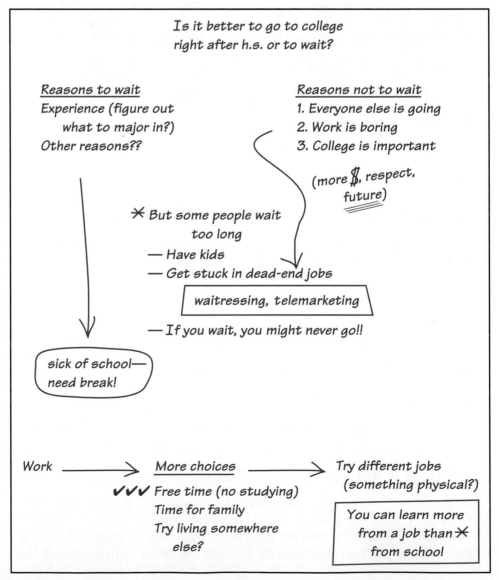

Brainstorming Notes

PRACTICE 3-5

Read Julia's brainstorming notes. How is her brainstorming similar to her freewriting (p. 57)? How is it different? Which ideas do you think she should write more about? Which ones should she cross out? Write your suggestions on the lines that follow.

_____

_____

_____

_____

_____

_____

PRACTICE 3-6

On a sheet of _unlined_ paper, brainstorm about why you decided to go to college. (Begin by writing "Why I decided to go to college" at the top of the page.) Write quickly, without worrying about being neat or using complete sentences. Try writing on different parts of the page, making lists, drawing arrows to connect related ideas, and starring important ideas. When you have finished, look over what you have written. Which ideas seem most interesting? Did you come up with any new ideas in your brainstorming that you did not think of in your freewriting?

FOCUS

Collaborative Brainstorming

You usually brainstorm on your own, but at times you may find it helpful to do **collaborative brainstorming**, working with other students to find ideas. Sometimes your instructor may ask you and another student to brainstorm together. At other times, the class might brainstorm as a group while your instructor records ideas. Whichever method you use, your goal is the same—to come up with as much material about your topic as you can.

PRACTICE 3-7

Brainstorm with three or four other students on the topic of why you decided to attend college. First, choose one person to write down ideas on a sheet of paper or on a section of the board. Then, discuss the topic informally. After about fifteen minutes, review all the ideas that have been listed. Has the group come up with any ideas that you can use in your writing? Be sure to keep a list of these ideas so that you can use them later on.

Clustering

Clustering, which is sometimes called *mapping*, is another strategy you can use to find ideas. When you cluster, you begin by writing your topic in the center of a sheet of paper. Then, you draw lines from the general topic to related ideas, moving from the center to the corners of the page. (These lines may look like spokes of a wheel or branches of a tree.) Your ideas will get more and more specific as you move from the center to the edges of the page.

When you finish clustering, you can cluster again on a new sheet of paper, this time beginning with a specific idea that you thought of the first time.

Here is Julia's clustering on the topic "Is it better to go to college right after high school or to wait?"

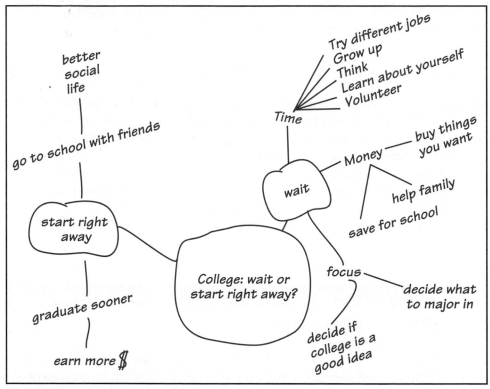

Clustering

PRACTICE 3-8

How is Julia's clustering similar to her brainstorming on the same subject (p. 58)? How is it different? Which branch of her cluster diagram do you think Julia should focus on when she writes her paragraph? Why? Should she add any other branches? Write your suggestions on the following lines. Then, discuss them with your class or in a small group of students.

_____

_____

_____

_____

_____

_____

_____

_____

_____

■ **PRACTICE 3-9** ▬▬▬▬▬▬▬▬▬▬▬▬▬

Try clustering on the topic "Why did you decide to go to college?"
Begin by writing this topic in the center of a sheet of unlined paper.
Circle the topic, and then draw branches to connect specific ideas
and examples, moving toward the edges of the page. When you have
finished, look over what you have written. Which ideas are the most
interesting? Which ones do you think you can write more about? Have
you come up with any new ideas that you did not discover during your
freewriting and brainstorming?

Journal Writing

A **journal** is a notebook or a computer file in which you record your
thoughts. It is also a place to record ideas that you might be able to write
about and a place where you can think about your assignments. In your
journal, you can do problem solving, try out sentences, keep track of details
and examples, and keep a record of interesting things you read or observe.

Once you have started writing regularly in your journal, try to go back
every week or so and reread what you have written. You may find ideas for
an assignment you are working on—or just learn more about yourself.

FOCUS

Journals

Here are some subjects you can write about in a journal:

- *Your school work* Writing regularly about the topics you are
  studying in school is one way to become a better student. For
  example, you can think on paper about what you are learning,
  write down questions about topics you are having trouble understanding, and examine new ideas.

- *Your job* You can write about the day-to-day triumphs and
  frustrations of your job. For example, you can write down conversations with coworkers, or you can list problems and remind
  yourself how you solved them. Rereading your journal may help
  you understand your strengths and weaknesses as an employee.

(continued on following page)

Journals, *continued from previous page*

- *Your ideas about your community and your world* As you learn more about the social and political world around you, you can explore your reactions to new ideas. For example, you may read an interesting story in the newspaper or see something on television or on the Internet that challenges your beliefs. Even if you are not ready to talk to others about what you are thinking, you can still "talk" to your journal.

- *Your impressions of what you see around you* Many writers carry their journals with them and record interesting, unusual, or funny things they notice as they go about their daily business. If you get into the habit of writing down your observations and reactions, you may be able to use them later in your writing.

- *Personal thoughts* Although you may not feel comfortable writing about your personal thoughts and experiences—especially if your instructor will read your journal—you should try to be as honest as you can. Writing about relationships with family and friends, personal problems, and hopes and dreams can help you get to know (and understand) yourself better.

Here is Julia's journal entry on the topic "Is it better to go to college right after high school or to wait?"

This is a hard topic for me to write about. When I finished high school, I never wanted to go to school again. High school was hard. I worked hard, but teachers always said I could do better. Studying was boring. I couldn't concentrate. I never seemed to get things right on homework or on tests. Things seemed easier for everyone else. Sometimes I hated school. So I decided I'd work and not go to college right away, or maybe ever. But after a year, here I am. I'm still not sure why. School always felt hard. Work was boring, but it was easy. For the first time, I could do everything right. I got raises and promotions and better hours because I was a good worker. I wasn't judged by how I did on some dumb test. For once, I had some self-esteem. So why am I here? Good question.

Journal Entry

■ PRACTICE 3-10

Set aside a time to write in your journal for fifteen minutes or so—during lunch, for example, or right before you go to bed—every day. Then, write your first journal entry. Being as honest with yourself as possible, try to explain why you really decided to go to college.

D Identifying Your Main Idea and Writing a Topic Sentence

When you think you have enough material to write about, it is time for you to identify your **main idea**—the central idea you will develop in your paragraph.

Begin by looking over what you have already written. As you read through your freewriting, brainstorming, clustering, and journal entries, look for the main idea that your material seems to support. The sentence that states this main idea and gives your writing its focus will be your paragraph's **topic sentence**.

The topic sentence of your paragraph is important because it tells both you and your readers what the focus of your paragraph will be. An effective topic sentence has three characteristics.

1. **A topic sentence is a complete sentence.** There is a difference between a *topic* and a *topic sentence*. The **topic** is what the paragraph is about.

    TOPIC   Whether to start college right after high school

    A **topic sentence**, however, is a complete sentence that includes a subject and a verb and expresses a complete thought.

    TOPIC SENTENCE   Students should not start college right after they finish high school.

2. **A topic sentence is more than just an announcement of what you plan to write about.** A topic sentence makes a point about the topic the paragraph discusses.

    ANNOUNCEMENT   In this paragraph, I will explain my ideas about whether students should go to college right after high school.

    TOPIC SENTENCE   My ideas about the best time to start college changed when I became a college student.

3. **A topic sentence presents an idea that can be discussed in a single paragraph.** If your topic sentence is too broad, you will not be able to discuss it in just one paragraph. If your topic sentence is too narrow, you will not be able to say much about it.

TOPIC SENTENCE TOO BROAD — Students have many different reasons for deciding whether to go to college right after high school.

TOPIC SENTENCE TOO NARROW — Most students begin college right after high school.

EFFECTIVE TOPIC SENTENCE — Students who begin college right after high school may be too immature to do well in school.

When Julia Reyes reviewed her notes, she saw that most of her material supported the idea that it was better to wait instead of starting college right after high school. She stated this idea in a topic sentence.

I think it's better to wait a few years instead of beginning college right after high school.

When Julia thought about how to express her topic sentence, she knew it had to be a complete sentence, not just a topic, and that it would have to make a point, not just announce what she planned to write about. When she reread the topic sentence she had written, she decided that it did these things and that it was neither too broad nor too narrow for her to support in a paragraph.

▰ PRACTICE 3-11 ▰

Read the following items. Put a check mark next to each one that you think would make an effective topic sentence for a paragraph.

Examples

Raccoons in the suburbs. _____

Raccoons often find food and shelter in suburban communities. ___✓___

1. The country's most exciting roller coasters. _____

2. Some of the country's most exciting roller coasters are made of wood.

   _____

3. It is dangerous to text while driving. _____

4. In this paragraph, I am going to write about texting while driving.

   _____

5. Reality shows can be addictive. _____

6. Some facts about reality shows. _____

PRACTICE 3-12

The following topic sentences are either too broad or too narrow. On the line after each sentence, write *Too broad* if the sentence is too broad and *Too narrow* if the sentence is too narrow. Then, rewrite each sentence—making it more specific or more general—so that it could be an effective topic sentence for a paragraph.

Examples

Eating in a restaurant is interesting.

Too broad. Possible rewrite: Eating in a Mexican restaurant is interesting

because there are many food choices.

I text my friends every day.

Too narrow. Possible rewrite: Texting is a good way to keep in touch with

friends.

1. The price of textbooks is very high.

   _____

   _____

2. At the supermarket, I can never find healthy snacks.

   _____

   _____

3. The United States is a beautiful country.

   _____

   _____

4. Everyone should be computer literate.

   _____

   _____

5. In some offices, workers can wear jeans and sneakers on casual Fridays.

   _____

   _____

■ **PRACTICE 3-13**

In Practices 3-3, 3-6, and 3-9, you practiced freewriting, brainstorming, and clustering. Now, you are ready to write a paragraph in response to the Seeing and Writing assignment on page 53.

   Why did you decide to go to college?

Your first step is to identify a main idea for your paragraph. Look over the work you have done so far, and decide what main idea your material can best support. On the lines below, write a topic sentence that expresses this idea.

Topic sentence: _____

_____

_____

E **Choosing Supporting Points**

After you identify your paragraph's main idea and state it in a topic sentence, review your notes again. Now, you are looking for specific details and examples to support your topic sentence. Write or type your topic sentence at the top of a sheet of paper. As you review your notes and continue to think about your topic, list all the supporting points you think you might be able to use in your paragraph.

   Julia listed the following points to support her paragraph's topic sentence. After she read through her list of points, she crossed out two points she did not want to write about.

TOPIC SENTENCE
(MAIN IDEA)
I think it's better to wait a few years instead of beginning college right after high school.
- Work experience
- Chance to earn money
- ~~Avoid friends from high school~~
- ~~Develop new hobbies~~
- Chance to develop self-esteem
- Time to grow up
- Chance to decide if college is right for you

■ **PRACTICE 3-14**

Now, continue to work on your own paragraph about why you decided to go to college. Reread your freewriting, brainstorming, and clustering exercises, and list below all the points you can use to support your topic sentence. (You can also list any new points you think of.)

Topic sentence: _____

_____

Supporting points:

- _____

- _____

- _____

- _____

- _____

F Arranging Your Supporting Points

Once you have listed all the supporting points you want to write about, arrange them in the order in which you plan to discuss them. Julia arranged her supporting points in the following list.

TOPIC SENTENCE I think it's better to wait a few years instead of beginning college right after high school.
1. Waiting gives people time to work and earn money.
2. Waiting gives people time to think about life and grow up.
3. Waiting helps people decide if college is right for them.
4. Waiting gives people a chance to develop self-esteem.

PRACTICE 3-15

Reread the points you listed in Practice 3-14 and cross out any points that you do not want to write about. On the following lines, arrange the remaining points in the order in which you plan to write about them.

1. _____

2. _____

3. _____

4. _____

G Drafting Your Paragraph

So far, you have found a main idea for your paragraph, written a topic sentence, listed supporting points, and arranged these points in the order in which you will write about them. Now, you are ready to write a first draft.

Begin drafting your paragraph by stating your topic sentence. Then, referring to your list of supporting points, write down your ideas without

worrying about correct sentence structure, word choice, spelling, or punctuation. If you think of a good idea that is not on your list, include it in your draft. (Don't worry at this point about where it fits or whether you will keep it.)

You can type your first draft, or you can write it by hand. Remember, though, that your first draft is a rough draft that you will revise. If you type your draft, leave extra space between lines. If you plan to revise on your handwritten draft, make things easy for yourself by leaving wide margins and skipping lines so you have room to add ideas.

When you have finished your rough draft, don't start revising it right away. Take a break, and then return to your draft and read it over very carefully.

Here is the first draft of Julia's paragraph on the topic "Is it better to go to college right after high school or to wait?"

Waiting

I think it's better to wait a few years instead of beginning college right

after high school. Many people start college right after high school just

because that's what everybody else is doing. But that's not always the

right way to go. Different things are right for different people. There are other

possible choices. Taking a few years off can be a better choice. During this

time, people can work and earn money. They also have time to think and grow

up. Waiting can even help people decide If college is right for them. Finally,

waiting gives them a chance to develop self-esteem. For all these reasons,

waiting a year or two between high school and college is a good idea.

Draft

PRACTICE 3-16

Read Julia's draft paragraph. What do you think she should change in her draft? What should she add? What should she take out? Write your suggestions on the following lines. Then, discuss your suggestions with the class or in a small group.

_____

_____

_____

_____

PRACTICE 3-17

Now, write a draft of your paragraph about why you decided to go to college, using the material you came up with for Practice 3-14. Be sure that your paragraph states your main idea in the topic sentence and that you support the topic sentence with specific points. When you have finished, give your paragraph a title that accurately reflects what you are writing about.

STRATEGIES FOR COLLEGE SUCCESS

Taking Advantage of Academic Advising

When deciding what courses to take and planning your schedule, you will need to consult your academic advisor. You may wish to keep your advisor's contact information and office hours in your address book. For additional tips on how to become a successful student, see Chapter 1.

H   Revising Your Paragraph

When you revise your work, you "re-see" it. **Revision** means much more than correcting a few commas or crossing out one word and putting another one in its place. Often, it means moving sentences around, adding words and phrases, and even changing the topic sentence. To get the most out of revision, begin by carefully rereading your draft—first aloud, then to yourself. Then, consider each of the questions on the checklist that follows.

> ✓ **Self-Assessment Checklist**
>
> ## Revising Your Paragraph
>
> ☐ Does your topic sentence clearly state your main idea?
>
> ☐ Do you have enough points to support your main idea?
>
> ☐ Have you included enough examples and details?
>
> ☐ Should you cross out any examples or details?
>
> ☐ Does every sentence say what you mean?
>
> ☐ Does the order of your sentences make sense?
>
> ☐ Is every word necessary?
>
> ☐ Have you used the right words?
>
> ☐ Does your paragraph include a concluding statement that sums up your main idea?

After Julia drafted the paragraph on page 68, she used the Self-Assessment Checklist above to help her revise her paragraph.

Waiting

For students who are not getting much out of school, it is often
~~I think it's~~ better to wait a few years instead of beginning college
                                                            away
right after high school. Many people start college right ~~after high school~~
              that is   *However, that is*
just because ~~that's~~ what everybody else is doing. ~~But that's~~ not always
              thing to do.
the right ~~way to go. Different things are right for different people.~~
                                                        often
~~There are other possible choices.~~ Taking a few years off can be a better
for college. Working at different jobs can help them decide on a career.
choice. During this time, people can work and earn money~~. They also have~~
Taking a year or two off also gives people
time to think and grow up. Waiting can even help people decide if college
  really   *Most important of all,*
is right for them. ~~Finally,~~ waiting gives them a chance to develop self-
              me,
esteem. For ~~all these reasons,~~ waiting a year ~~or two~~ between high school
                  was
and college ~~is~~ a good idea/, *and I think it can be a good idea for other*

students, too.

┌ *I was a poor student in high school.*
School always felt hard. When I took a year off,
everything changed. In high school, I always saw
all the things I couldn't do. At work, I learned what
I could do. Now, I think I can succeed.

Revised Draft

When she revised her paragraph, Julia crossed out sentences, added sentences, and changed the way she worded her ideas. Her biggest change was adding an explanation of how taking a year off had helped her. She also revised her topic sentence to reflect the broader perspective her personal experience gave her. Here is the final version of her revised paragraph.

Waiting

For students who are not getting much out of school, it is often better to wait a few years instead of beginning college right after high school. Many people start college right away just because that is what everybody else is doing. However, that is not always the right thing to do. Taking a few years off can often be a better choice. During this time, people can work and earn money for college. Working at different jobs can help them decide on a career. Taking a year or two off also gives people time to think and grow up. Waiting can even help people decide if college is really right for them. Most important of all, waiting gives them a chance to develop self-esteem. I was a poor student in high school. School always felt hard. When I took a year off, everything changed. In high school, I always saw all the things I couldn't do. At work, I learned what I could do. Now, I think I can succeed. For me, waiting a year between high school and college was a good idea, and I think it can be a good idea for other students, too.

Topic sentence

Support

Concluding statement

FOCUS

Editing

Don't confuse revision with editing, which comes *after* revision. When you **edit**, you check for correct grammar, punctuation, mechanics, and spelling. Then, you proofread your writing carefully for typing errors that a computer spell checker may not identify. You also make sure that you have indented the first sentence of your paragraph and that every sentence begins with a capital letter and ends with a period.

Remember, editing is a vital last step in the writing process. Readers may not take your ideas seriously if your writing includes errors in grammar or spelling.

PRACTICE 3-18

Read the final version of Julia's revised paragraph (above), and compare it with her first draft (p. 68). What specific changes did she make? Which do you think are her best changes? Why? Answer these questions on the following lines. Then, with the class or in a small group, discuss your reaction to the revised paragraph.

_____

_____

_____

_____

_____

_____

▉ PRACTICE 3-19 ▉

Use the Self-Assessment Checklist on page 70 to help you evaluate
the paragraph you drafted for Practice 3-17. What else can you add
to support your topic sentence? Should anything be crossed out? Can
anything be stated more clearly? On the following lines, list some of the
changes you might make in your draft.

_____

_____

_____

_____

_____

✓ Seeing and Writing: Skills Check

Look back at your response to the Seeing and Writing activity on
page 53. Consider the following questions:

- Does your paragraph contain any information that is not
  necessary?
- Does your paragraph contain any material that needs to be
  rewritten?
- Does your paragraph need any additional information?

Then, revise your paragraph, adding, crossing out, and rewording
material as needed. (You can use the Self-Assessment Checklist on
p. 70 to help you revise.) Finally, edit your paragraph, checking
grammar, punctuation, mechanics, and spelling—and proofread
carefully for typing errors.

✓ Review Checklist

Writing a Paragraph

☐ Be sure you understand paragraph structure. (See 3A.)

☐ Consider your assignment, purpose, and audience. (See 3B.)

(continued on following page)

Review Checklist, *continued from previous page*

☐ Use different strategies—freewriting, brainstorming, clustering, and journal writing—to help you find ideas to write about. (See 3C.)

☐ Identify your main idea, and write a topic sentence. (See 3D.)

☐ Choose supporting points from your notes. (See 3E.)

☐ Arrange your supporting points in a logical order. (See 3F.)

☐ Write a draft of your paragraph. (See 3G.)

☐ Revise and edit your draft. (See 3H.)

Fine-Tuning Your Paragraph

WORD POWER

spectacle: a public performance or show; an unusual sight

festival: a day or period of celebration

commemoration: a celebration in which a person or an event is remembered

SEEING AND WRITING ▲

The picture above shows the Feast of San Gennaro, a festival held every year in the Little Italy neighborhood of New York City. Look at the picture, and then write a paragraph about an event that you wanted to attend but could not. What was special about the event? What caused you to miss it? Try to use the Word Power words in your paragraph.

A Writing Unified Paragraphs

A paragraph is **unified** when all its sentences support the main idea stated in the topic sentence.

Paragraph Map: Writing Unified Paragraphs

Topic sentence _____

_____

Support for main idea _____

_____

Support for main idea _____

_____

Support for main idea _____

_____

Concluding statement _____

_____

A paragraph is **not unified** when its sentences do not all support the main idea in the topic sentence. When you revise, you can make your paragraphs unified by crossing out sentences that do not support your topic sentence. Then, if necessary, you can add some sentences that do support the topic sentence.

The following paragraph is not unified because it includes details that do not support the topic sentence.

Paragraph Not Unified

Applying for a Loan

Although applying for a loan can be confusing, the process is not all that difficult. The first step is to determine which bank has the lowest interest rate. There are a lot of banks in my neighborhood, but they aren't very friendly. The last time I went into one, I waited for twenty minutes before anyone bothered to talk to me. Once you have chosen a bank, you have to go to the bank in person and apply, and if the bank isn't friendly, you don't want to go there. This is a real problem when you apply for a loan. If you have any questions about the application, you won't be able to get anyone to answer them. After you have submitted the application comes the hard part—waiting for approval.

The following revised paragraph is unified. When the writer reread his paragraph, he deleted the sentences that did not support his topic sentence. Then, he added some sentences that did.

Unified Paragraph

Applying for a Loan

<u>Although applying for a loan can be confusing, the process is not all that difficult.</u> The first step is to determine which bank has the lowest interest rate. ~~There are a lot of banks in my neighborhood, but they aren't very friendly. The last time I went into one, I waited for twenty minutes before anyone bothered to talk to me.~~ Although a half-percent difference in rates may not seem like much, over the course of a four-year loan, the savings can really add up. Once you have chosen a bank, you have to go to the bank in person and apply~~, and if the bank isn't friendly, you don't want to go there.~~ ~~This is a real problem when you apply for a loan. If you have any questions about the application, you won't be able to get anyone to answer them.~~ Make sure you tell the loan officer exactly what rate you are applying for. Then, take the application home and fill it out, being careful not to omit any important information. If you have any problems with your credit, explain them on the application or in a separate letter. When the application is complete, take it back to the bank, and ask any questions you might have. (Do not sign the application until all your questions have been answered.) After you have submitted the application comes the hard part — waiting for approval.

— Hector de la Paz (student)

Margin labels:
Irrelevant information deleted
Support added
Irrelevant information deleted
Support added

PRACTICE 4-1

Underline the topic sentence in each of the following paragraphs. Keep in mind that the topic sentence may not be the first sentence of the paragraph.

Example

 <u>Learning to drive was very difficult for me.</u> My father wanted to teach me to drive, but he didn't have time. My older brother said he would do it. We used his car, which had a stick shift. This made it a lot harder to learn to drive. He took me to a big, empty parking lot so that I wouldn't crash into anything. I practiced how to start the car. When I got the car started, I had trouble shifting to the next gear. The engine kept stalling again and again. My brother yelled at me, and I felt stupid. After a while, he let me take the car on the road. It was hard to shift and steer at the same time. Whenever I stopped for a red light, the car jerked and stalled. As I practiced, I eventually got the hang of it. Finally, I passed my driving test, and now I am a good driver.

1. The Innocence Project arranges for lawyers and law students to help free innocent people who have been wrongly convicted. Sometimes, a DNA test can prove that these people are innocent, but this testing is often not done. The test is expensive, and prisoners cannot afford it. Unfortunately, they have no other way to prove their innocence, except to hope that the Innocence Project will choose their cases. The lawyers and law students in the Innocence Project study the cases and take those they think they can win. As a result of the Innocence Project, more than 170 people in the United States have been released from jail. Fourteen of these people had been sentenced to death. Thousands of other prisoners are waiting and hoping that they will be released from jail as a result of the work of the Innocence Project.

2. Most adults went to public schools when they were young. They sat in rows, listened to the teacher, and went to recess with many other children. At the end of the day, they went home to their families. These days, many children are home schooled. Instead of going to school, they stay home and learn. Usually, the mother is the teacher. She may order books and materials on the Internet. She teaches all the subjects to her children. Although some people worry that home-schooled children do not interact enough with people outside their family, many of these home-schooled children do well once they get to college.

3. What were your parents thinking when they gave you your name? Did they give you a popular name? If so, other children in your class probably had the same name. Some popular names change over time. Biblical names have been popular for boys for many years. In recent years, for example, the top boys' names have come from the Bible—Jacob, Michael, and Joshua. Girls' names are different. In the past, many girls were named Mary, but recently some of the most popular girls' names have been Emily, Emma, and Madison. Today, girls are often named after characters from books, movies, or television shows. Most likely, your name is a name that was popular when you were born.

PRACTICE 4-2

The following paragraph has no topic sentence. Read it, and then choose the best topic sentence from the list below.

People cheat on taxes, people cheat on their spouses, and people cheat on their insurance claims. People cheat on this, and they cheat on that. They skim a little off the top here and add a little over there. No one seems to be playing by the rules anymore. It's time we started challenging people for their dishonesty. What does all this cheating say about our society? Maybe it says that we're incapable of succeeding honorably. Maybe it suggests that honesty is just for people who don't understand how the world works. When we cheat or accept the fact that someone else cheats, we are really only cheating ourselves. In the long run, we have to live with the problems that cheating creates and pay the price for our dishonesty.

Put a check mark next to the topic sentence that best expresses the main idea in the paragraph above.

1. Everyone, regardless of age or gender, seems to be cheating. _____

2. Cheating is bad for society. _____

3. The widespread cheating in our society has to stop. _____

4. Lots of people cheat. _____

5. There is nothing we can do to stop the cheating that we see around us. _____

PRACTICE 4-3

The following paragraphs do not have topic sentences. Think of a topic sentence that sums up each paragraph's main idea, and write it on the line above the paragraph.

Example

Books can be banned from schools and libraries for various reasons.

_____

Each year, the American Library Association puts out a list of the books that people want removed from libraries and classrooms. Books like *The Catcher in the Rye* by J. D. Salinger and *Forever* by Judy Blume have been challenged for sexual content and offensive language. The Harry Potter series by J. K. Rowling is often criticized for supposedly encouraging witchcraft. Books like *Daddy's Roommate* have been challenged for promoting homosexuality. Finally, *The Adventures of Huckleberry Finn* by Mark Twain has been challenged for being racist.

1. _____

_____

Until the 1960s, wearing a hat was a mark of adulthood. It was a more formal time when many men wore suits and hats even at sports events. For women, dresses, white gloves, and hats were essential for many occasions. By 1960, though, going hatless was more common. Many people resisted the formal look of the past and began to dress much more casually. They abandoned their suits, dresses, white gloves, and hats. Going bareheaded became the rule except on very special occasions. Even though designers have often predicted that hats are coming back in style, this hasn't happened yet.

2. _____

Tupperware, a type of plastic food storage container, was first sold in 1951 at home parties. In a friend's living room, housewives would be invited to check out the various sizes and shapes of the plastic storage containers with the famous "burping" seal. They would pick the ones they wanted and order them from the Tupperware consultant—a housewife like them. Today, you can still find Tupperware parties in some places, but so many women work outside the home that they need other ways to buy Tupperware. Shopping malls may have Tupperware showcases—booths where shoppers can purchase Tupperware. Shoppers can also buy Tupperware online, directly from the company. They may even get an email invitation to an online party, where they can buy Tupperware.

3. _____

_____

_____

A mystery shopper goes to a store, checks it out, and completes a questionnaire about its prices, customer service, cleanliness, and other things that affect a customer's experience. Typical locations for mystery shopping are department stores, supermarkets, restaurants, and bars. As a result of the shopper's report, the store might improve its staff training or lower its prices to be more competitive. Most mystery shoppers earn between $12 and $20 for a shopping trip of less than an hour. They usually work part-time. It is not a very highly paid job, but for someone who likes to shop, it might be perfect.

PRACTICE 4-4

Read the following paragraphs. Underline the topic sentence of each paragraph. Then, check to see if every sentence in the paragraph supports that topic sentence. Write *unified* after the paragraphs that are unified and *not unified* after the ones that are not unified.

Example

Pet ownership is a big responsibility. Thousands of families adopt dogs and cats every month. Other family activities include taking vacations and playing sports together. In fact, families who spend time together tend to be happier and communicate more. Most people give little thought to their pets' needs for a proper diet, exercise, company, and veterinary care. In fact, few people realize how much time and money they will spend taking care of their pets. ___*not unified*___

1. Drivers must be careful to avoid road rage incidents. Road rage occurs when a driver loses control over his or her emotions in a stressful situation. Driving in bad weather can be very stressful. A car does not handle as easily on snowy or icy roads as it does on dry ones. Snow tires can make winter driving safer. Even with snow tires, though, driving on

slippery roads requires concentration. Road rage can lead to property damage and even injury. Therefore, drivers should always keep their emotions under control. _____

2. Music can either help or hurt a person's ability to recall information. For example, students who study while listening to loud dance music tend to remember less than those who study in quiet settings. The reason for this is that dance music has a strong rhythm, which tends to distract a person from the material being studied. Classical music, on the other hand, may help improve memory. Research shows that some people remember information more clearly if they listen to quiet classical music while studying. Understanding the link between music and memory can help students make wise choices about listening to music while studying. _____

3. Georgia O'Keeffe was a bold and influential painter. Her most famous paintings are of flowers and of scenes from the Southwest. Many tourists visit the Southwest to enjoy its beautiful deserts. Taos, New Mexico, is an especially busy tourist spot. O'Keeffe developed a unique painting style. She created dramatic images that went against the artistic fashion of her times. In fact, her rich use of color has inspired many artists. Quite a few artists today work in video and collage as well as in paint. O'Keeffe's work is on display in many of the world's leading museums. _____

▨ PRACTICE 4-5 ▨

Review the paragraphs in Practice 4-4 that you decided were not unified. Reread the topic sentence of each paragraph. Then, cross out the sentences in each paragraph that do not support the topic sentence.

Example

Pet ownership is a big responsibility. Thousands of families adopt dogs and cats every month. ~~Other family activities include taking vacations and playing sports together. In fact, families who spend time together tend to be happier and communicate more.~~ Most people give little thought to the animals' needs for a proper diet, exercise, company, and veterinary care. In fact, few people realize how much time and money they will spend taking care of their pets.

1. Drivers must be careful to avoid road rage incidents. Road rage occurs when a driver loses control over his or her emotions in a stressful situation. Driving in bad weather can be very stressful. A car does not handle as easily on snowy or icy roads as it does on dry ones. Snow tires can make winter driving safer. Even with snow tires, though, driving on slippery roads requires concentration. Road rage can lead to property damage and even injury. Therefore, drivers should always keep their emotions under control.

2. Music can either help or hurt a person's ability to recall information. For example, students who study while listening to loud dance music tend to remember less than those who study in quiet settings. The reason for this is that dance music has a strong rhythm, which tends to distract a person from the material being studied. Classical music, on the other hand, may help improve memory. Research shows that some people remember information more clearly if they listen to quiet classical music while studying. Understanding the link between music and memory can help students make wise choices about listening to music while studying.

3. Georgia O'Keeffe was a bold and influential painter. Her most famous paintings are of flowers and of scenes from the Southwest. Many tourists visit the Southwest to enjoy its beautiful deserts. Taos, New Mexico, is an especially busy tourist spot. O'Keeffe developed a unique painting style. She created dramatic images that went against the artistic fashion of her times. In fact, her rich use of color has inspired many artists. Quite a few artists today work in video and collage as well as in paint. O'Keeffe's work is on display in many of the world's leading museums.

■ PRACTICE 4-6

On the lines below, write a paragraph that develops the main idea that is stated in each topic sentence. After you finish, check to make sure that each paragraph is unified.

1. Many people don't pay their bills on time. _____

_____

_____

_____

_____

2. My neighborhood is an interesting place. _____

_____

_____

_____

_____

3. If I were president of this college, I would make a few changes.

_____

_____

_____

_____

_____

B Writing Well-Developed Paragraphs

A paragraph is **well developed** when it includes enough specific details and examples to support the topic sentence.

Paragraph Map: Writing Well-Developed Paragraphs

Topic sentence _____

_____

Support (details and examples) _____

_____

Support (details and examples) _____

_____

Support (details and examples) _____

_____

Concluding statement _____

_____

The amount of support you need depends on the scope of the idea you state in your topic sentence. If your topic sentence is relatively limited, then two or three well-chosen examples may be enough to support: My school's registration process has three problems. If your topic sentence is more open-ended and broader in scope, however, then you will have to include more support: The plans for the new sports stadium are seriously flawed.

FOCUS

Developing Paragraphs with Details and Examples

Specific details and examples can make a paragraph convincing. For example, in a paragraph on a history test, you could say that many soldiers were killed during the American Civil War. Your paragraph would be far more effective, however, if you said that over 500,000 soldiers were killed during the Civil War—more than in all the other wars in U.S. history combined.

The following paragraph is not well developed because it does not give readers specific information about why bottled water is bad for the environment (which is what the topic sentence promises).

Paragraph Not Well Developed

Bottled Water and the Environment

Bottled water is harmful for the environment. A surprising amount of fuel goes into making and transporting the bottles. The environmental problems do not end when the water has been delivered. Fortunately, more consumers today are choosing tap water.

In the following revised paragraph, the writer added details and examples that help readers understand the point made in the topic sentence.

Well-Developed Paragraph

Bottled Water and the Environment

Bottled water is harmful for the environment. A surprising amount of fuel goes into making and transporting the bottles. For example, manufacturing the bottles uses about 1.5 million barrels of oil each year. Getting the bottled water from factories to stores requires an additional 500,000 gallons of oil per year. The environmental problems do not end when the water has been delivered. Almost 90 percent of the plastic bottles are not recycled after use. These bottles do not degrade, so they clog the nation's landfills. Fortunately, more and more consumers are becoming aware of these problems and are choosing tap water.

— Fatima Ibrahim (student)

Details and Examples Support Topic Sentence

NOTE: Length is no guarantee that a paragraph is well developed. A paragraph that contains one generalization after another can be quite long and still not provide enough support.

PRACTICE 4-7

Some of the following paragraphs are well developed; others are not. On the line after each paragraph, write *well developed* if the paragraph is well developed and *not well developed* if it is not.

Example

The National Spelling Bee has many purposes. It encourages children to improve their spelling, vocabulary, and English usage. As a result, children can read and write better and get higher scores on standardized tests. Spelling bees also encourage friendly competition among children and their schools. *not well developed*

1. PlumpyNut can help starving people survive. PlumpyNut is peanut-based paste that was invented by a French scientist in 1999. It comes in a foil wrapper and does not need to be refrigerated. PlumpyNut is a high-energy, high-protein food that can save people's lives. Before PlumpyNut came into use, the most common nutritious food given to starving people was based on powdered milk. However, this milk-based food needed clean water and careful preparation by medical staff. PlumpyNut is much simpler to use. It can be fed to a child by a parent. The contents of the foil packet can be used after it has been opened. PlumpyNut is truly a life-saver. _____

2. Jeans have a long history. They were invented by Levi Strauss in 1873. Strauss had a dry goods store in San Francisco. One of his customers kept ripping his pants, so Strauss made pants that would be stronger. He got a patent on his invention, and blue jeans were born. At first, they were called "waist overalls." In the 1960s, the term "jeans" became popular. Today, there are many kinds of jeans sold by many different companies. _____

3. Oprah's Book Club has put many new and classic books on the best-seller list. In 1996, Oprah Winfrey started her book club, which recommends books that she has chosen. She chooses books that deal sympathetically with real human problems. She has picked books by Nobel Prize winners as well as new books by previously unknown authors. Most of the books on her list have become very popular with readers.

_____

■ PRACTICE 4-8

The following paragraphs are not well developed. On the lines below each paragraph, write three questions or suggestions that might help the writer develop his or her ideas more fully.

Example

Adam Sandler is a great comedian. Some of his movies are absolutely hilarious. He is especially good at using funny voices to express his emotions. I never get tired of watching Adam Sandler's movies. I have seen *The Waterboy* and *Funny People* several times each.

- *Describe the voices Adam Sandler uses.* _____

- *Describe the roles he plays in one of the movies mentioned.* _____

- *Tell about the funny way he talks in these movies.* _____

1. For me, having a regular study routine is important. I need to do the same things at the same times. If I have important school work to do, I stick to my routine. As long as I follow my schedule, everything works out all right.

- _____

- _____
- _____

2. Religion is a deeply personal issue. Attitudes toward religion vary from person to person. One person I know considers religion an essential part of life. Another feels just the opposite. Because of such differences, it is impossible to generalize about religious attitudes.

- _____
- _____
- _____

PRACTICE 4-9

Choose one of the paragraphs from Practice 4-8. Reread it, and review your suggestions for improving it. Then, rewrite the paragraph, adding specific details and examples to make it well developed.

_____
_____
_____
_____
_____
_____
_____
_____

STRATEGIES FOR COLLEGE SUCCESS

Proofreading Your Work

After running a spell check, proofread your work to catch typos such as *if* for *is* or *mush* for *much*. For additional tips on how to become a successful student, see Chapter 1.

C Writing Coherent Paragraphs

A paragraph is **coherent** when all its sentences are arranged in a definite order. In general, you can arrange the ideas in a paragraph in three ways— in *time order*, in *spatial order*, or in *logical order*.

Time Order

You use **time order** to arrange events in the order in which they occurred. News reports, historical accounts, and process explanations are usually arranged like this.

Paragraph Map: Writing Coherent Paragraphs (Time Order)

Topic sentence _____

_____

First, _____

_____

Next, _____

_____

Finally, _____

_____

Concluding statement _____

_____

The following paragraph presents events in time order. (Transitional words and phrases are underlined.)

Ralph Ellison

No other American writer achieved as great a reputation on the basis of a single book as Ralph Ellison did. Ellison was born <u>in 1914</u> in Oklahoma City, Oklahoma, and grew up in the segregated South. <u>In 1936</u>, he came to New York City to earn money to pay his tuition at Tuskegee Institute, where he was a senior majoring in music. <u>After</u> becoming friends with many writers who were part of the Harlem Renaissance—a flowering of art, music, and literature among African Americans—he decided to remain in New York. <u>During this period</u>, Richard Wright, author of *Native Son* and *Black Boy*, encouraged Ellison to write his first short story. <u>In the years that followed</u>, Ellison published two collections of essays and some short fiction. <u>Eventually</u>, in 1952, he wrote *Invisible Man*, the novel that established him as a major twentieth-century writer.

— Mike Burdin (student)

WORD POWER

renaissance: a rebirth or revival

Notice that throughout the paragraph, the writer uses transitional words and phrases that signal time order—*in 1914, in 1936, after, during this period, in the years that followed,* and *eventually.* These words and phrases help to make the paragraph coherent.

Some Transitional Words and Phrases That Signal Time Order			
after	finally	soon	dates (for example,
afterward	first . . . next	still	"in 1920")
at first	later	then	times (for example,
before	meanwhile	today	"at 8 o'clock,"
during	now	until	"that night")
earlier	recently	when	
eventually	since	while	

■ PRACTICE 4-10

Read the following paragraphs, whose sentences are organized in time order. Underline the transitional words and phrases that make each paragraph coherent.

Example

Writing a research paper requires several steps. First, you must choose a topic to write about. The topic should be broad enough to allow for an interesting discussion but narrow enough to cover in a few pages. Next, begin researching your topic. Reference works, books, articles, and Web sites are all good places to look for information. While you are gathering material, you might adjust your topic on the basis of what you are learning about it. When you have finished collecting information, it is time to plan your paper by drafting an outline. Then, it is time to write and to revise. Finally, you will want to add a bibliography or works-cited page and proofread your paper.

1. A job interview is most likely to go well when you are prepared for it. The first step is to determine your strengths. Do you have the right level of education for the job? Are you experienced in the field? What special skills do you have? The next step is to research the company and the kind of business it does. If you have a thorough knowledge of the company, you will make a good impression and be able to answer many questions. Finally, decide what points you want to emphasize in the interview. Although the interviewer will guide the conversation, you should be ready to offer your own thoughts as well.

2. Filmmaker Spike Lee has had a successful career making unusual movies. Before he started making movies professionally, he was a film student at New York University. In 1986, he released his first feature film, *She's Gotta Have It*. Critics praised this low-budget movie for its strong characters and clever dialogue. Then, Lee went on to make such acclaimed movies as *Do the Right Thing, Jungle Fever,* and *Malcolm X*. In these movies, he explored issues of race in America. Recently, he made *When the Levees Broke*, a documentary about Hurricane Katrina, and *Inside Man*, a film about a bank robbery. What many people do not realize is that Lee writes, produces, directs, and even acts in many of his films.

■ **PRACTICE 4-11**

The following paragraph includes no transitional words and phrases to connect its ideas. Read the paragraph carefully. Then, after consulting the list of transitional words and phrases on page 87, add appropriate transitions to connect the paragraph's ideas in time order.

A Killer Disease

The worst pandemic in the history of the world occurred in 1918, when the flu killed between 20 and 40 million people. _____, soldiers in American military camps began to get sick during their training for combat in World War I. _____, as military units moved from one battlefield to another in Europe, the disease spread from soldier to soldier. _____, it started to spread to civilians. _____, the war ended, and as people came together to celebrate, they continued to spread the flu. _____, the flu attacked people all over the world, especially young people who had previously been healthy. _____, doctors were trying desperately to find ways to treat their flu patients, but nothing worked. To stop the spread of the disease, gauze masks and quarantines were tried, but these efforts had little effect. _____, millions of people all over the world were dying. _____, we are still learning more about the 1918 flu.

■ **PRACTICE 4-12**

Arrange the following sentences into a coherent paragraph. Be sure you are able to explain why you arranged the sentences the way you did. (Begin by identifying the paragraph's main idea.)

____ **1.** During colonial times, public voice votes were common.

____ **2.** Soon, all voters may be able to cast ballots on the Internet.

____ **3.** Voting machines, which ensured privacy and accuracy, were common by the early 1900s.

____ **4.** Then, around the time of the Revolutionary War, voting became a private matter with the use of secret paper ballots.

____ **5.** Until the late 1800s, political parties printed and distributed their own ballots.

_____ **6.** Voting methods in the United States have changed dramatically in the past 250 years.

_____ **7.** Recently, voting officials have used computers to count votes.

Spatial Order

You use **spatial order** to present details in relation to one another—from top to bottom, from right to left, from far to near, and so on. Spatial order is used most often in paragraphs that describe something—for example, in a lab report describing a piece of equipment.

Paragraph Map: Writing Coherent Paragraphs (Spatial Order)

Topic sentence _____

_____

In front of _____

_____

Next to _____

_____

Behind _____

_____

Concluding statement _____

_____

The following paragraph uses spatial order. (Transitional words and phrases are underlined.)

My Greatgrandmother's House

When I was fourteen, my family and I traveled to Michigan to visit the town where my great-grandmother had lived. Somerset was hardly a town; in fact, it was just a collection of farms and cow pastures. Scattered through the fields were about twenty buildings. One of them was my great-grandmother's old brick farmhouse, which was sold after she died. Next to the house were a rusting silo and a faded barn. In front of the house was a long wooden porch that needed painting. On the porch were a potted plant, two white wooden rocking chairs, and a swing. The house was locked, so all we could do was walk around it and look. The lace curtains that my great-grandmother had made before she died still hung in each window. In back of the house was a small cemetery that contained eight graves. <u>There</u>, off <u>in the corner</u>, on the oldest-looking stone, was the name "Azariel Smith"—the name of my great-grandmother's father.

— Molly Ward (student)

Notice how transitional words and phrases that signal spatial order—*next to, in front, on the porch, in back, there,* and *in the corner*—help make the paragraph coherent.

Some Transitional Words and Phrases That Signal Spatial Order

above	below	inside	on/to the right
along	beneath	near	outside
around	beside	next to	over
at/on the top	in	on the bottom	there
at/on the bottom	in back (of)	on the top	under
behind	in front (of)	on/to the left	within

■ PRACTICE 4-13

Read the following paragraphs, whose details are arranged in spatial order. Underline the transitional words and phrases that make each paragraph coherent.

Example

My childhood home was a typical one-story house. The front door opened into a small foyer. <u>Above</u> the foyer and <u>to the right</u> was a carpeted living room shaped like the letter *L.* The short part of the *L* served as our dining room. <u>Behind</u> the living room was the kitchen. A hallway led from the kitchen to a bathroom <u>on the right</u> and then to two bedrooms. <u>Below</u> the bedrooms was a playroom. At the other end of the first floor, <u>beneath</u> the living room, was a garage.

1. Visitors to the White House in Washington, D.C., tour rooms that are decorated in a variety of styles and that serve a variety of functions. For example, in front of the Visitors' Entrance is the Library, furnished in the style of the Federal period (1800–1820). To the left of the Library is the Vermeil Room, decorated in gold and silver and used occasionally as a women's lounge. To the right and front of the Library is the East Room, traditionally used for large gatherings, such as concerts and press conferences. Next to the East Room is the Green Room, a drawing room decorated in delicate shades of green. Beside the Green Room is the Blue Room, an oval-shaped room used as a reception area. From the Blue Room, visitors enter the Red Room, decorated in the French Empire style. These and other public rooms give visitors a sense of the beauty and history of the White House.

2. The most spectacular sight I have ever seen is Machu Picchu, an ancient Incan city in Peru. Machu Picchu is built high on a ridge in the Andes Mountains. Below it is the Urabamba River that runs swiftly north and raises a white mist. Behind Machu Picchu, the mountain Huayna Picchu stands like an enormous dark guard. Its triangular faces look like arrowheads pointing to the sky. All around Machu Picchu, thick brush covers the land, including the steps cut into the mountain. These steps were used for growing crops. To me, however, they seem to have been carved for giants to walk on. Within the city of Machu Picchu, houses and temples are made of carved stones. In the center of the city is the main plaza, where one of my favorite sites, the Temple of the Three Windows, is located. Inside this temple, tourists can look out of three large stone windows and see the mountains beyond. I do not need photographs to remember the view from this temple. It will always be with me.

PRACTICE 4-14

The following paragraph includes no transitional words and phrases to connect ideas. Read the paragraph carefully. Then, after consulting the list of transitional words and phrases on page 90, add appropriate transitions to connect the paragraph's ideas in spatial order.

Scrapbooking: A Popular Hobby

Many people are now saving, collecting, and arranging their memorabilia in scrapbooks. The scrapbook is usually a hard-covered album, which can be 8½ x 11 inches or smaller. _____, the pages are made of special paper that does not fade or weaken over time. A typical page might have, _____, a person's name in fancy letters. _____ the name might be a group of photographs of that person at some unforgettable life events, such as playing on a winning soccer team or celebrating a special birthday. _____ of a page, a scrapbook might feature glitter or colored tape outlining a high school or college graduation program. _____, there might be some photographs of the graduate in his or her cap and gown. _____ of the page, fancy ribbons might surround prom tickets. Scrapbooks give people a way to collect their treasured memories in a creative and long-lasting way.

WORD POWER
memorabilia: objects valued for their personal significance

■ **PRACTICE 4-15**

Arrange the following sentences into a coherent paragraph. Be sure you are able to explain why you arranged the sentences the way you did. (Begin by identifying the paragraph's main idea.)

___ **1.** Next to the video gallery is a display of celebrity portraits.

___ **2.** For example, in front of the museum, on the main lawn, officials have installed a brightly colored fountain.

___ **3.** In a small gallery to the left of the entrance hall, videotapes made by artists play on three monitors.

___ **4.** The Middletown Museum of Art includes several displays designed to attract younger visitors.

___ **5.** Inside the main doors is the large entrance hall, with a dozen large, spinning mobiles hanging from the ceiling.

___ **6.** Officials hope young people will wander behind and above the entrance hall toward the rest of the museum's art exhibits.

___ **7.** Behind the fountain, a series of small animal sculptures leads toward the main doors.

Logical Order

You use **logical order** to indicate why one idea logically follows another—for example, to move from the least important idea to the most important one. Logical order is used most often in paragraphs that provide information or in paragraphs with a persuasive purpose—for example, in a paragraph trying to convince readers to get an annual flu shot.

Paragraph Map: Writing Coherent Paragraphs (Logical Order)

Topic Sentence _____

_____

One reason _____

_____

Another reason _____

_____

The most important reason _____

_____

Therefore, _____

_____

Concluding statement _____

_____

The following paragraph presents ideas in logical order. (Transitional words and phrases are underlined.)

Priorities

As someone who is both a parent and a student, I have had to develop strategies for coping. For example, I try to do my studying at night after I have put my son to bed. I want to give my son all the attention that he deserves, so after I pick him up from day care, I play with him, read to him, and watch a half hour of TV with him. When I am sure he is asleep, I begin doing my schoolwork. I also try to use every spare moment that I have during the day. For instance, if I have an hour between classes, I go to the computer lab and do some work. While I eat lunch, I get some of my reading out of the way. When I ride home from work on the bus, I review my class notes. Most important, I always keep my priorities in mind. My first priority is my son, my second priority is my schoolwork, and my last priority is keeping my apartment clean.

— Vanessa Scully (student)

The writer of this paragraph moves from her least important to her most important point. Notice how transitional words and phrases that signal logical order—*for example, also, for instance,* and *most important*—help make the paragraph coherent.

Some Transitional Words and Phrases That Signal Logical Order

also	furthermore	not only . . . but also
consequently	in addition	one . . . another
equally important	in conclusion	similarly
first . . . second . . . third	in fact	the least important
for example	last	the most important
for instance	moreover	therefore
for one thing		

PRACTICE 4-16

Read the following paragraphs, whose sentences are organized in logical order. Underline the transitional words and phrases that make the paragraphs coherent.

Example

Among the many reasons to support school sports, the most important is the education students get on the playing field. Students in a sports program such as basketball or track learn teamwork, self-confidence, and the value of physical fitness. They <u>also</u> feel a sense of belonging that athletes on a team enjoy. <u>In addition</u>, schools often benefit financially from the sales of tickets to sporting events. Attending a football game may help provide students with new textbooks and other materials. <u>The least important</u> reason to support school sports is the chance that a student athlete might go on to become a famous sports figure. Such success is extremely rare, and young people should be encouraged to pursue other, more practical careers.

1. Even though only one out of every ten people is left-handed, "lefties" have a surprising amount of influence on our society. For one thing, five of the last seven presidents were left-handed. In addition, one in four of the Apollo astronauts was left-handed. Also, computer whizzes Steve Jobs and Bill Gates are both left-handed, along with many of their employees at Apple and Microsoft. Moreover, left-handed people are disproportionately represented among Nobel Prize winners. Researchers who have tried to explain this phenomenon have discovered some interesting facts. For example, left-handed people seem to have high IQs. Moreover, many left-handers are good at big-picture and visual thinking. For this reason, they may be able to see things in ways that right-handers cannot. In conclusion, it appears that many left-handed people excel both because they are smart and because—in the words of the Apple slogan—they "think different."

2. I have made some important decisions lately. For example, last year I decided to move from my home in rural Connecticut to an apartment in New York City. This move has had many benefits. For instance, being in the city gave me more career opportunities. It also helped me to meet many more people than I could have in my small Connecticut town. Furthermore, I found plenty of interesting things to do with my time. My new interests include Thai cooking and salsa dancing. In fact, I find the cultural mix in the city interesting and exciting.

■ PRACTICE 4-17

The following paragraph includes no transitional words and phrases to connect ideas. Read the paragraph carefully. Then, after consulting the list of transitional words and phrases on page 93, add appropriate transitions to connect the paragraph's ideas in logical order.

Showing Support

Wearing an awareness bracelet can be a way to show support for

a team, a political opinion, or a charitable cause. _____ use of

awareness bracelets is to show support for a sports team. _____,

fans of the Boston Celtics basketball team wear green awareness bracelets. _____, supporters of the Boston Red Sox baseball team can show their loyalty by wearing red bracelets. Awareness bracelets can _____ express political views. _____, there are bracelets for those who support the Democratic and Republican parties. There is even a bracelet for people who oppose global warming. _____, people can wear awareness bracelets to support a worthy charity. _____, there are special bracelets for victims of the tsunami in Southeast Asia, of Hurricane Katrina, and of the genocide in Darfur, Sudan. Because awareness bracelets also make a fashion statement, many young people have adopted this method of expressing their views.

▉ PRACTICE 4-18 ▉

Arrange the following sentences into a coherent paragraph. Be sure you are able to explain why you arranged the sentences the way you did. (Begin by identifying the paragraph's main idea.)

_____ **1.** With this victory, Rankin became one of the first women in the world elected to a governing body.

_____ **2.** Jeanette Rankin had one of the most unusual political careers in American history.

_____ **3.** As a result of this vote, Rankin lost her bid for election to the Senate in 1918, but she remained active in peace issues.

_____ **4.** Although this constitutional amendment passed the House, it was defeated in the Senate and not enacted until 1919.

_____ **5.** In 1916, four years before American women had the right to vote, she won a seat in Congress.

_____ **6.** While in Congress, Rankin helped draft a constitutional amendment to give women the right to vote.

_____ **7.** In 1940, after being reelected to Congress, Rankin cast her vote against U.S. entry into World War II.

_____ **8.** Perhaps Rankin's most important act was her vote against U.S. entry into World War I.

_____ **9.** In conclusion, Rankin is remembered as someone who stood by her principles, regardless of the cost to her career.

_____ **10.** By doing so, Rankin became the only member of Congress to vote against U.S. entry into both world wars.

✓ **Seeing and Writing: Skills Check**

Look back at your response to the Seeing and Writing activity on page 74. Reread it, and answer the following questions:

- Is your paragraph unified?
- Is your paragraph well developed?
- Is your paragraph coherent?

Then, revise and edit your paragraph.

CHAPTER REVIEW

EDITING PRACTICE

Read the following student paragraphs, and evaluate each one in terms of its unity, development, and coherence. First, underline the topic sentence. Next, cross out any sentences that do not support the topic sentence. Then, add transitional words and phrases where needed. Finally, discuss in class what additional details and examples might be added to each paragraph and what titles might be suitable for each.

Anne Bonny and Mary Read

eBay Home Page

1. At a young age, pirate Anne Bonny traded a life of wealth and privilege for one of adventure and crime. In 1716, she ran away from home to marry a sailor. Sailors passed through the place where she lived, on the East Coast of the United States, on a regular basis. Later, she met a pirate named Calico Jack Rackham. Bonny soon left her husband to join Rackham's crew. She developed a reputation as a fierce fighter. In 1720, Bonny met another female pirate named Mary Read. They were captured by authorities. Bonny, who was pregnant, was not sentenced to death because executing a pregnant woman was against the law. Read received a death sentence. Before it could be carried out, she died of a fever in prison. No one knows what finally became of Bonny.

2. People should know certain things before they start to sell any thing on eBay. They have to register and open an eBay account. They can sell clothes, furniture, jewelry, electronic devices, cars, toys, or almost anything else. They should fill out a form that describes the item, the

price, the shipping cost, and the method of payment. If the sale is successful, the sellers will receive an email from eBay. They will have to pay eBay a fee to sell each item. This fee is based on the item's value. They will have to pay eBay a fee based on the item's selling price. When receipt of payment is confirmed, they can ship the items to the buyers.

3. NASCAR, which stands for the National Association for Stock Car Auto Racing, sponsors one of the most popular sporting events in the United States. Years ago, NASCAR events used to be held mainly in the South. To lower the risks of terrible accidents, NASCAR drivers have to wear special seat belts and restraints for the head and neck. Races take place all over the country, including New Hampshire, Delaware, Nevada, and California. The biggest race of the season is the Daytona 500. In 1979, it was the first stock car race to be televised from start to finish. NASCAR drivers are famous among race fans. Dale Earnhardt Jr. and Jeff Gordon are extremely popular. Fans follow the careers of their favorite drivers and sometimes spend an entire week at the race-track, cheering on their favorites as they prepare for a big race.

Cars at a NASCAR Race

COLLABORATIVE ACTIVITIES

1. Working in a group, list some distractions that make it hard for students to perform well in college. Arrange these distractions from least important to most important. Then, create a topic sentence that states the main idea suggested by your list. Finally, draft a paragraph in which you discuss why some students have difficulty succeeding in college.

2. Think of a place you know well. Write a paragraph that describes the place so that readers will be able to imagine it. Decide on a specific spatial order—for example, outside to inside, left to right, or front to back. When you have finished, trade paragraphs with another student. See if you can sketch the place described in your partner's paragraph. If you cannot, offer suggestions that could improve his or her description.

3. Bring to class a paragraph from a newspaper, magazine, or Web site. Working in a group of three students, underline each paragraph's topic sentence. Then, decide whether each paragraph is unified, well developed, and coherent. If it is not, work together to make it more effective.

✓ **Review Checklist**

Fine-Tuning Your Paragraph

☐ A paragraph is unified when it focuses on a single main idea, which is stated in the topic sentence. (See 4A.)

☐ A paragraph is well developed when it contains enough specific details and examples to support the main idea. (See 4B.)

☐ A paragraph is coherent when its sentences are arranged in a definite order and it includes all necessary transitional words and phrases. (See 4C.)

Exemplification

CHAPTER 5

PREVIEW

In this chapter, you
will learn to write
an exemplification
paragraph.

SEEING AND WRITING ▲

The picture above shows the cast members from the television show
Lost, a TV series that followed the lives of survivors of a plane crash
on a mysterious tropical island. Look at the picture, and then write
a paragraph in which you discuss what skills you would need to
survive on a deserted island. Try to use the Word Power words in your
paragraph.

WORD POWER

adversity: difficulty

improvise: to make do, to
manage

marooned: stranded

In Chapters 3 and 4, you learned how to write effective paragraphs. In Chapters 5 through 13, you will learn different ways of organizing your ideas within paragraphs.

A   What Is Exemplification?

What do we mean when we say that an instructor is *good* or that a football team is *bad*? What do we mean when we say that a particular government policy is *misguided* or that a particular war was *wrong*? To clarify general statements like these, we use **exemplification**—that is, we give **examples**, specific instances that illustrate a general idea.

General Statement	*Specific Examples*
Today is going to be a hard day.	Today is going to be a hard day because I have a history test in the morning and a lab quiz in the afternoon. I also have to go to work an hour earlier than usual.
My car is giving me problems.	My car is burning oil and won't start on cold mornings. In addition, I need a new set of tires.

ASSIGNMENTS FOR EXEMPLIFICATION

You will use exemplification in many of your college classes. Here are some typical assignments:

- *In a psychology class:* What are the typical signs of excesssive jealousy?
- *In an environmental studies class:* How does "green cleaning" help improve the environment?
- *In a religion course:* What roles does religion play in public life?

An **exemplification paragraph** explains or clarifies a general idea—stated in the topic sentence—by providing specific examples. Personal experiences, class discussions, observations, conversations, and reading can all be good sources of examples. An exemplification paragraph contains the following elements:

- An exemplification paragraph begins with a topic sentence that clearly states the main idea of the paragraph.
- The topic sentence is followed by examples that support the general statement made in the topic sentence.
- Examples are arranged in **logical order**—for example, from least important to most important or from general to specific.
- The paragraph closes with a concluding statement that sums up its main idea.

Paragraph Map: Writing an Exemplification Paragraph

Topic sentence _____

_____

Example #1 _____

_____

Example #2 _____

_____

Example #3 _____

_____

Concluding statement _____

_____

The following paragraph uses examples to make a point about state lotteries.

The Trouble with Lotteries

Even for states that are financially troubled, lotteries are a bad way to raise money. First, lotteries can create financial problems for all but the few people who win. For example, in states that have lotteries, the average player spends nearly $150 each year on tickets. Some even spend $500 or more. Because the odds of winning are low, much of this money is wasted. Second, state lotteries send the message that gambling is risk-free and acceptable. Specifically, ticket buyers may ask themselves, "If the government sponsors gambling, how bad can it be?" They may therefore be less likely to see the possible dangers. Finally, lotteries are not necessarily a good or consistent revenue source. For instance, states spend millions of dollars on prizes and advertising for lotteries. These costs eat into the money that is made. Furthermore, lotteries are not immune to economic downturns. For example, some states saw double-digit drops in ticket sales during the recent recession. For these reasons, lotteries are a big gamble for states and their citizens.

— Jeffrey Smith (student)

- Topic sentence
- Transitions introduce examples
- Concluding statement

When you write an exemplification paragraph, be sure to include appropriate transitional words and phrases. These transitions will indicate how one example is related to another as well as how each example supports the topic sentence.

Some Transitional Words and Phrases for Exemplification

also	furthermore	the most important
finally	in addition	example
first . . . second . . .	moreover	the next example
(and so on)	one example . . .	
for example	another example	
for instance	specifically	

GRAMMAR IN CONTEXT

Exemplification

When you write an exemplification paragraph, always use a comma after the introductory transitional word or phrase that introduces your examples.

> First, lotteries can create financial problems for all but the few people who win.
> Second, state lotteries send the message that gambling is risk-free and acceptable.
> Finally, lotteries are not necessarily a good or consistent revenue source.

For information on using commas with introductory transitional words and phrases, see 31B.

B Writing an Exemplification Paragraph

PRACTICE 5-1

Read this exemplification paragraph, and answer the questions that follow it.

The Little World of Matchbox Cars

Matchbox cars are tiny die-cast models that come in a wide variety of styles. The most common Matchbox models, the ones most often seen in toy stores, are about 2.5 inches long. There are also larger cars, called "Major" or "Super Kings." Because Majors are unusual and fairly expensive, they are usually bought by collectors. Matchbox does not restrict itself to making model cars. For instance, the company has made airplanes called "Sky Busters" that it sold in stores and supplied to the major airlines. Matchbox has also made a series of fantasy vehicles called "Ultra Heroes." In addition to these items, Matchbox makes double-decker buses, helicopters, and trucks as well as play sets that include fire stations and car washes. Because of this wide variety of models, people who like Matchbox cars have no trouble finding new and unusual items to buy.

— Michael Graham (student)

1. Underline the topic sentence of the paragraph.

2. List the specific examples the writer uses to support the topic sentence. The first example has been listed for you.

   Small cars that are found in toy stores

   _____

   _____

   _____

3. Circle the transitional words and phrases that the writer uses to connect examples in the paragraph.

4. Underline the paragraph's concluding statement.

STRATEGIES FOR COLLEGE SUCCESS

Using Examples in Your Class Notes

When you take notes, include examples to illustrate key concepts. The examples will help you remember what the instructor was talking about. For instance, if your history professor is explaining *direct democracy*, write down the term, its definition, and an example (such as "California ballot propositions"). For additional tips on how to become a successful student, see Chapter 1.

■ PRACTICE 5-2

Following are four topic sentences for exemplification paragraphs. After each sentence, list three examples that could support the main idea. For example, if you were writing about the poor quality of food in your school cafeteria, you could list mystery meat, weak coffee, and stale bread.

1. Many of the skills learned by our grandparents are not needed in today's high-tech world.

_____

_____

_____

2. People who want to get their news from the Internet have many options.

_____

_____

_____

3. I have always been very unlucky (or lucky) in love.

_____

_____

_____

4. Although many people criticize television shows as mindless, there are a few exceptions.

_____

_____

_____

▮ PRACTICE 5-3

Choose one of the following topics.

Why social networking is important to you

The importance of family in your life

A memorable book or movie

The benefits of a healthy diet

How not to act at a party

How a service at your school could be improved

The accomplishments of someone you admire

Your favorite sports team

Violence in movies or video games

The demands of being a parent

Drivers who are a menace

Trends on your college campus

Exercise for busy people

The best jobs for a recent college graduate

The consequences of putting things off

Problems you face daily

PRACTICE 5-4

Use one or more of the strategies discussed in 3C to help you come up with examples for the topic you have chosen.

PRACTICE 5-5

Review your notes from Practice 5-4, and list below the four or five examples that can best help you develop a paragraph on the topic you have chosen.

- _____
- _____
- _____
- _____
- _____

PRACTICE 5-6

Reread your list of examples from Practice 5-5. Then, draft a topic sentence that states your paragraph's main idea.

Topic sentence: _____

_____

PRACTICE 5-7

On the lines below, arrange the examples you listed in Practice 5-5 in a logical order—for example, from least important to most important.

1. _____
2. _____
3. _____
4. _____
5. _____

PRACTICE 5-8

Draft your exemplification paragraph.

PRACTICE 5-9

Using the Self-Assessment Checklist below, revise your exemplification paragraph.

PRACTICE 5-10

Print out a final draft of your exemplification paragraph.

✓ Seeing and Writing: Skills Check

Look back at your response to the Seeing and Writing activity on page 99. Reread it, and answer the following questions:

- Is your paragraph unified?
- Is your paragraph well developed?
- Is your paragraph coherent?

Then, revise and edit your paragraph.

✓ Self-Assessment Checklist

Writing an Exemplification Paragraph

☐ Does the topic sentence clearly state the main idea of your paragraph?

☐ Do all your examples support your topic sentence?

☐ Have you used enough examples?

☐ Have you used appropriate transitional words and phrases?

☐ Have you put commas after the transitional words or phrases that introduce your examples?

☐ Have you included a concluding statement that sums up your paragraph's main idea?

CHAPTER REVIEW

1. The following student exemplification paragraph is missing a topic sentence, transitional words and phrases, and a concluding statement. After reading the paragraph, fill in the missing elements on the appropriate lines below. (Look on p. 102 for a list of transitions.)

Preparing a Résumé: What Not to Do

_____

_____. _____, people should

never exaggerate on a résumé. Employers can usually spot exaggerations. They

know that "food professional" at a fast-food restaurant means that a person was

flipping hamburgers or working at the counter. _____, people should

not be vague about their accomplishments. For instance, they shouldn't just say

that they saved the company money or that they have management experience.

Instead, they should include the exact amount of money they saved or the specific

management duties they performed. _____, people should never try

to cover up gaps in their employment history. They should not invent jobs or lie

about the amount of time they worked. Instead, they should explain any gaps in a

cover letter. _____

_____

2. Create an exemplification paragraph by adding examples that support the topic sentence below. Connect the examples with appropriate transitions, and end the paragraph with a clear concluding statement. Finally, add an appropriate title on the line provided.

_____

Shoppers can do a number of things to make sure they get the

most for their money. _____

_____

_____

_____

_____

_____

_____

WORD POWER

public service: a service performed for the benefit of the public

3. The billboard pictured below shows a Mothers Against Drunk Drivers (MADD) public service advertisement. Look carefully at the picture. Then, write an exemplification paragraph explaining how this advertisement gets its point across to its audience. Begin your paragraph with a topic sentence that states the point you want to make about the ad. Then, give examples to support your topic sentence.

Narration

PREVIEW

In this chapter, you will learn to write a narrative paragraph.

SEEING AND WRITING ▲

The picture above shows a bride and groom with their family after a wedding on a beach. Look at the picture, and then write a paragraph in which you tell the story of how this couple met and how they decided where their wedding should be held. Try to use the Word Power words in your paragraph.

WORD POWER

commitment: devotion or dedication

sentimental: overly romantic

A What Is Narration?

Narration is writing that tells a story by presenting a sequence of related events. Effective narratives include vivid details that make the story come alive for readers. The more specific the details are, the better the narrative will be.

ASSIGNMENTS FOR NARRATION

You will use narration in many of your college classes. Here are some typical assignments:

- *In an education class:* Discuss an experience you remember from your student teaching that reinforced your decision to become a teacher.
- *In an introduction to literature course:* Write an alternative ending for James Joyce's short story "Araby."
- *In a criminal justice class:* What events enabled the government to build its criminal case against the Gambino crime family?

A **narrative paragraph** tells a story about what happened to you or to someone else. It can be something that actually happened, or it can be fictional. All the details in the narrative should relate to the main point of the paragraph. A narrative paragraph contains the following elements:

- A narrative paragraph begins with a topic sentence that states the main idea of the paragraph—that is, why you are telling the story.
- The topic sentence is followed by the events that are necessary to tell the story.
- A narrative paragraph presents events in a definite **time order**, usually the order in which they actually occurred.
- The paragraph ends with a concluding statement that sums up the main idea stated in the topic sentence.

Paragraph Map: Writing a Narrative Paragraph

Topic sentence _____

_____

Event #1 _____

_____

Event #2 _____

_____

Event #3 _____

_____

Concluding statement _____

_____

The following paragraph relates events that support the point that the fashion designer Chloe Dao had a difficult life.

Overnight Success

Chloe Dao traveled a difficult road to become a successful fashion designer. When Dao was a baby, her parents decided to leave her native country, Laos, and come to the United States. Unfortunately, the Viet Cong captured her and her family as they tried to cross the border. They were sent to a refugee camp, where they stayed for four years. In 1979, when she was eight, Dao and her family were allowed to come to the United States. Now, they had to earn enough money to live. Dao's mother worked three jobs. On the weekends, the entire family ran the snack bar at a flea market. Finally, they saved enough money to open a successful dry-cleaning business. When she was twenty, Dao moved to New York to attend school. After she graduated, she got a job as production manager for designer Melinda Eng. Eventually, she opened a boutique, where she sold clothes that she designed. Her big break came in 2006 when she was chosen as a finalist on the reality show *Project Runway*. Although Chloe Dao may appear to be an "overnight success," she had to struggle to get where she is today.

— Christine Clark (student)

Topic sentence

Transitions link events in time order

Concluding statement

As you arrange your ideas in your narrative paragraphs, be sure to use clear transitional words and phrases. These signals help readers follow your narrative by indicating the order of the events you discuss.

Some Transitional Words and Phrases for Narration

after	first . . . second . . .	(for example, "two days,"
as	third	"five minutes,"
as soon as	immediately	"ten years")
before	later	soon
by this time	later on	suddenly
dates (for example,	meanwhile	then
"in 2006")	next	when
earlier	now	while
eventually	phrases that identify	
finally	specific times	

Narration

When you write a narrative paragraph, you tell a story. As you become involved in your story, you might begin to string events together without proper punctuation. If you do, you will create a **run-on**, an error that occurs when two sentences are joined incorrectly.

INCORRECT (RUN-ON)	Dao's mother worked three jobs on the weekends, the entire family ran the snack bar at a flea market.
CORRECT	Dao's mother worked three jobs. On the weekends, the entire family ran the snack bar at a flea market.

For information on how to identify and correct run-ons and comma splices, see Chapter 20.

B Writing a Narrative Paragraph

PRACTICE 6-1

Read this narrative paragraph, and answer the questions that follow it.

Breaking the Color Barrier

Jackie Robinson challenged racial prejudice throughout his life. Early on, his African American family experienced discrimination in their wealthy, mostly white neighborhood. Robinson was not discouraged. Growing up, he excelled at every sport he played. After the United States entered World War II, Robinson enlisted in the army. While serving in the army, he was ordered to the back of a military bus because of his race. He refused, and soon after, he was disciplined. However, he later received an honorable discharge. After leaving the army, Robinson played baseball in the Negro Leagues. These leagues were the only option for African American players following the racial separation of U.S. baseball in 1889. He did so well that he was recruited to play for the Brooklyn Dodgers, thus officially breaking the color barrier. Some white teammates and fans complained, but Robinson did not let them interfere with his playing. His performance helped the Dodgers win the National League pennant. Eventually,

Robinson helped his team win the World Series. Meanwhile, he argued for the broader participation of African Americans in big-league sports. By the time of his death in 1972, Robinson had become the first African American to be inducted into the Baseball Hall of Fame. His achievements in the face of racial prejudice have made him a hero to many Americans.

— Carmen Alvos (student)

1. Underline the topic sentence of the paragraph.

2. List the major events of the narrative. The first event has been listed for you.

   Robinson's family experienced discrimination.

   _____

   _____

   _____

   _____

   _____

   _____

   _____

   _____

   _____

   _____

   _____

3. Circle the transitional words and phrases that the writer uses to link events in time.

4. Underline the paragraph's concluding statement.

STRATEGIES FOR COLLEGE SUCCESS

Staying Organized

Buy a wall calendar and an organizer. Keep the calendar at home, and carry the organizer with you. Update both throughout the semester by writing in project due dates, exam dates, appointments and reminders, and so on. For additional tips on how to become a successful student, see Chapter 1.

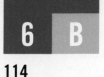

PRACTICE 6-2

Following are four topic sentences for narrative paragraphs. After each topic sentence, list four events you could include in a narrative paragraph to support the main idea. For example, if you were telling about a dinner that turned out to be a disaster, you could tell about how the meat burned, the vegetables were overcooked, and the guests arrived late.

1. The day started out normally enough, but before it was over, my life had changed forever.

   _____

   _____

   _____

   _____

2. When I was young, my grandmother told me a story about her childhood.

   _____

   _____

   _____

   _____

3. I'll never forget my first best friend.

   _____

   _____

   _____

   _____

4. It was a difficult decision for me to make.

   _____

   _____

   _____

   _____

PRACTICE 6-3

Choose one of the following topics (or a topic of your own).

A happy time

Your proudest moment

A frightening event

A family story

A conflict with authority

A new experience

An injustice you experienced

An embarrassing moment

A favorite holiday memory

A challenge you faced and overcame

A risk you took

A coincidence

An unexpected gift

A great loss

A lesson you learned

An experience that caused you to grow up

▦ PRACTICE 6-4

Use one of the strategies in 3C to help you come up with events and details for the topic you have chosen in Practice 6-3.

▦ PRACTICE 6-5

Review your notes from Practice 6-4, and list below four or five events that could help you develop a narrative paragraph on the topic you have chosen.

- _____

- _____

- _____

- _____

- _____

▦ PRACTICE 6-6

Reread your list of events from Practice 6-5. Then, draft a topic sentence that states your paragraph's main idea.

Topic sentence: _____

_____

▦ PRACTICE 6-7

On the lines below, arrange the events you listed in Practice 6-5 in the order in which they occurred.

1. _____

2. _____

3. _____

4. _____

5. _____

 PRACTICE 6-8

Draft your narrative paragraph.

 PRACTICE 6-9

Using the Self-Assessment Checklist below, revise your narrative paragraph.

 PRACTICE 6-10

Print out a final draft of your narrative paragraph.

✓ **Seeing and Writing: Skills Check**

Look back at your response to the Seeing and Writing activity on page 109. Reread it, and answer the following questions:

- Is your paragraph unified?
- Is your paragraph well developed?
- Is your paragraph coherent?

Then, revise and edit your paragraph.

✓ **Self-Assessment Checklist**

Writing a Narrative Paragraph

☐ Does your topic sentence state your paragraph's main idea?

☐ Do your sentences move clearly from one event to another?

☐ Have you included enough details to make the story come alive for readers?

☐ Have you used appropriate transitional words and phrases?

☐ Have you avoided run-on sentences as you presented events in your narrative?

☐ Have you included a concluding statement that sums up your paragraph's main idea?

CHAPTER REVIEW

1. The following student narration paragraph is missing a topic sentence, transitional words and phrases, and a concluding statement. After reading the paragraph, fill in the missing elements on the appropriate lines below. (See p. 111 for a list of transitions.)

The Date from Hell

_____

_____

The date started when I picked Tracy up at her apartment. _____ we

left, I had to get the approval of her roommates. Apparently, I passed the test.

_____ we drove to a small Italian restaurant that I like. _____

the owner tried to seat us, Tracy said that she didn't like the table. _____,

she found a table she liked. _____, we sat down and ordered. When

the food came, Tracy sent it back because she said it wasn't what she had

expected. When the waiter brought her another platter, she sent it back

because she said it was too cold. _____, dinner was over, and we

went back to her apartment to talk. We didn't agree about anything. I told her

I liked a certain movie, and she said she didn't. I told her who I voted for in

the last election, but she voted for another person. If I had an opinion about

anything, she had the opposite opinion. _____, I had had enough.

I told Tracy that I had to get up early the next morning, and I went home.

_____

_____

2. Create a narrative paragraph by adding events to support the topic sentence below. Connect the events with appropriate transitions, and end the paragraph with a clear concluding statement that sums up the main idea. Finally, add an appropriate title on the line provided.

_____

When I was young, I had a very unusual ambition. _____

_____

_____

_____

_____

_____

_____

_____

_____

_____

_____

_____

_____

3. The picture below shows two people, surrounded by various objects. Look carefully at the picture, and then write a narrative paragraph that tells the story of the people in the picture. Begin your paragraph with a topic sentence that states the main idea of your paragraph. In the rest of the paragraph, present the events that support your topic sentence. Make sure the events are arranged in clear time order.

Description

PREVIEW

In this chapter, you will learn to write a descriptive paragraph.

SEEING AND WRITING ▲

The picture above shows a building in Barcelona, Spain, designed by the famous architect Antoní Gaudi. Study the picture carefully, and then write a paragraph that describes what you see. Include enough specific details so that readers will be able to "see" the scene you are describing without looking at the picture. Try to use the Word Power words in your paragraph.

WORD POWER

elaborate: rich in detail

exotic: foreign, unusual

ornate: excessively ornamented; flowery

119

A What Is Description?

When you write a **description**, you use language that creates a vivid impression of what you have seen, heard, smelled, tasted, or touched. The more specific details you include, the better your description will be.

ASSIGNMENTS FOR DESCRIPTION

You will use description in many of your college classes. Here are some typical assignments:

- *In an art history class:* Study Marc Chagall's painting *I and the Village*, and describe the images you see.
- *In a meteorology class:* Describe the destruction caused by the storm surge during the Galveston hurricane of 1904.
- *In a social work class:* Write a profile of the family you observed during your service-learning experience.

The following description is flat because it includes no specific details.

FLAT DESCRIPTION

Today I saw a beautiful sunrise.

In contrast, the description below is full of details that convey the writer's experience to readers.

RICH DESCRIPTION

Early this morning, as I walked along the sandy beach, I saw the sun rise slowly out of the ocean. At first, the ocean looked red. Then, it turned slowly to pink, to green, and finally to blue. As I stood watching the sun, I heard the waves hit the shore, and I felt the cold water swirl around my toes. For a moment, even the small grey and white birds that hurried along the shore seemed to stop and watch the dazzling sight.

The revised description relies on sight (*saw the sun rise slowly out of the ocean; looked red; turned slowly to pink, to green, and finally to blue*), touch (*the sandy beach; felt the cold water*), and sound (*heard the waves hit the shore*).

FOCUS

Description

Vague, overused words—such as *good, nice, bad,* and *beautiful*—do not help readers see what you are describing. When you write a descriptive paragraph, try to use specific words and phrases that make your writing come alive.

A **descriptive paragraph** paints a picture of a person, place, or object. A descriptive paragraph contains the following elements:

- A descriptive paragraph should have a topic sentence that states the main idea of your paragraph.
- The topic sentence should be followed by the details that support the topic sentence.
- Details are arranged in a definite **spatial order**, the order in which you observed the scene you are describing—for example, from near to far.
- The paragraph ends with a concluding statement that sums up the main idea stated in the topic sentence.

Paragraph Map: Writing a Descriptive Paragraph

Topic sentence _____

_____

Detail #1 _____

_____

Detail #2 _____

_____

Detail #3 _____

_____

Concluding statement _____

_____

The following paragraph uses descriptive details to support the idea that the Lincoln Memorial is a monument to American democracy.

The Lincoln Memorial

The Lincoln Memorial was built to celebrate American democracy. In front
of the monument is a long marble staircase that leads from a reflecting pool
to the Memorial's entrance. Thirty-six columns surround the building. Inside
the building are three rooms. The first room contains the nineteen-foot-tall
statue of Lincoln. Seated in a chair, Lincoln looks exhausted after the long
Civil War. One of Lincoln's hands is a fist, suggesting his strength, and the
other is open, suggesting his kindness. On either side of the first room are
two other rooms. On the wall of one room are the words of the Gettysburg

Topic sentence

**Transitions link details
in spatial order**

Address. On the wall of the other room, Lincoln's Second Inaugural Address is displayed. Above the Gettysburg Address is a mural that shows an angel freeing the slaves. Above the Second Inaugural Address is another mural, which shows the people of the North and the South coming back together.

Concluding statement

As its design shows, the Lincoln Memorial was built to celebrate both the sixteenth president and the nation's struggle for equality.

— Nicole Lentz (student)

As you arrange your ideas in a descriptive paragraph, be sure to use appropriate transitional words and phrases. These signals will lead readers from one detail to another and will indicate the order in which you are discussing them.

Some Transitional Words and Phrases for Description		
above	in front of	on top of
behind	inside	outside
below	nearby	the first . . . the second
between	next to	the next
beyond	on	under
in	on one side . . .	
in back of	on the other side . . .	

GRAMMAR IN CONTEXT

Description

When you write a descriptive paragraph, you sometimes use **modifiers**—words and phrases that describe another word or group of words.

A modifier should be placed as close as possible to the word it is supposed to modify. If you place modifying words or phrases too far from the words they modify, you create a **misplaced modifier** that will confuse readers.

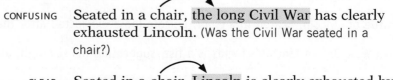

CONFUSING   Seated in a chair, the long Civil War has clearly exhausted Lincoln. (Was the Civil War seated in a chair?)

CLEAR   Seated in a chair, Lincoln is clearly exhausted by the long Civil War.

For information on how to identify and correct misplaced modifiers, see Chapter 24.

B Writing a Descriptive Paragraph

■ PRACTICE 7-1 ■■■■■■■■

Read this descriptive paragraph, and answer the questions that follow it.

Morning on the Bus

Early this morning, the people on the bus were strangely quiet. When the doors to the bus opened, I saw that it was almost empty. Inside the bus, way in the back, two people who were coming home from a night of clubbing were sleeping. Nearby, I saw a small woman dressed in a black and white waitress uniform. She held a paper container of coffee in both hands and looked out the window into the soft morning light. At the next stop, several people boarded the bus. They slumped down in their seats, closed their eyes, and tried to catch a few more minutes of sleep. At the front of the bus, a short, unshaven man took out a newspaper, folded it so that only a small bit was showing, and tried to read. As I watched him, I realized that he was reading the same page again and again. The only sounds were the engine and the screeching of the brakes as the bus came to a stop. No one was really awake yet. It was as if everyone was quietly waiting for the day to start.

— Caitlin McNally (student)

1. Underline the topic sentence of the paragraph.

2. What are some of the details the writer uses to describe the people on the bus? The first detail has been listed for you.

   Two people coming home

   _____

   _____

   _____

3. List some of the transitions the writer uses to lead readers from one detail to another.

   _____

   _____

   _____

4. Underline the paragraph's concluding statement.

■ PRACTICE 7-2

Following are four topic sentences for descriptive paragraphs. After each topic sentence, list three details that could help convey why you are writing the description. For example, to describe an interesting person, you could tell what the person looked like, how he or she behaved, and what he or she said.

1. It was a long hike, but when we finally got to the top of the mountain, the view was incredible.

   _____

   _____

   _____

2. Every community has a house that all the kids think is haunted.

   _____

   _____

   _____

3. In every living situation, there is one person who is an unbelievable slob.

   _____

   _____

   _____

4. I'll never forget the first time I did something really risky.

   _____

   _____

   _____

■ PRACTICE 7-3

Choose one of the following topics (or a topic of your own) as the subject of a descriptive paragraph.

A famous person

A place you dislike

A favorite spot on campus

An unusual person

Your dream house

A friend or family member

A work of art

An object you couldn't live
without

Your workplace

Your favorite article of clothing

Your favorite teacher

Someone you see every day

A building you find interesting

Your car, truck, or bike

Something you would like to have

An accident scene

Someone you admire

A fashion disaster

■ PRACTICE 7-4

Use one or more of the strategies discussed in 3C to help you come
up with specific details about the topic you have chosen. If you can,
observe your subject directly, and list your observations.

■ PRACTICE 7-5

Review your notes from Practice 7-4, and list below some details that
could help you develop a descriptive paragraph on the topic you have
chosen.

- _____
- _____
- _____
- _____
- _____
- _____

■ PRACTICE 7-6

Reread your list of details from Practice 7-5. Then, draft a topic sentence
that summarizes your paragraph's main idea.

Topic sentence: _____

_____

■ PRACTICE 7-7

On the lines below, arrange the details you listed in Practice 7-5. You
might arrange them in the order in which you look at the subject—for
example, from left to right, near to far, or top to bottom.

1. _____
2. _____
3. _____
4. _____
5. _____
6. _____

■ PRACTICE 7-8

Draft your descriptive paragraph.

■ PRACTICE 7-9

Using the Self-Assessment Checklist below, revise your descriptive paragraph.

■ PRACTICE 7-10

Print out a final draft of your descriptive paragraph.

✓ Seeing and Writing: Skills Check

Look back at your response to the Seeing and Writing activity on page 119. Reread it, and answer the following questions:

- Is your paragraph unified?
- Is your paragraph well developed?
- Is your paragraph coherent?

Then, revise and edit your paragraph.

✓ Self-Assessment Checklist

Writing a Descriptive Paragraph

- ☐ Does your topic sentence state the paragraph's main idea?
- ☐ Do all your details support your topic sentence?
- ☐ Are your details specific enough to give readers a picture of your subject?
- ☐ Have you used appropriate transitional words and phrases?
- ☐ Have you placed modifying words and phrases clearly?
- ☐ Have you included a concluding statement that sums up your paragraph's main idea?

CHAPTER REVIEW

1. The following student descriptive paragraph is missing a topic sentence, transitional words and phrases, and a concluding statement. After reading the paragraph, fill in the missing elements on the appropriate lines below. (See p. 122 for a list of transitions.)

Disaster Area

_____

_____

When I open the door to her room, the clutter is overwhelming. Directly

_____ the room, under the windows, is my sister's desk. Surprisingly,

this is the neatest, most organized part of her room. _____ side of

her desk is a large blue dictionary. Next to that are two large white loose-

leaf binders. _____ side of the desk is her iPod dock and a small

television set. On another wall is my sister's bed. It is almost always unmade

and covered with clothes, books, magazines, an empty bag of potato chips,

a half-eaten sandwich, and three or four stuffed animals. _____

the bed is her dresser. Usually, the drawers are open, and their contents are

draped over the front of the drawers. If she has had a particularly bad time

deciding what to wear, the floor will be covered with clothes. _____

of the dresser is a jumbled collection of make-up, perfume bottles, hair spray,

brushes, cotton balls, at least one hairdryer, and several empty soda cans.

_____

_____

2. Create a descriptive paragraph by adding details to support the topic sentence below. Connect details with appropriate transitions, and end the paragraph with a clear concluding statement that sums up the main idea. Finally, add an appropriate title on the line provided.

_____

My picture in my high school yearbook reveals a lot about me.

_____

_____

_____

_____

_____

_____

_____

_____

_____

_____

_____

_____

_____

_____

_____

_____

3. The picture below shows a beachfront hotel in South Beach, a resort area in Miami Beach, Florida. Look carefully at the picture, and write a descriptive paragraph for a brochure that advertises the hotel. Begin with a topic sentence that states the main idea of your paragraph. Then, in the rest of the paragraph, supply specific details about the hotel's location and facilities. Your goal is to persuade prospective customers to stay at the hotel.

Process

PREVIEW

In this chapter, you will learn to write a process paragraph.

SEEING AND WRITING ▲

The picture above shows someone trying to fix a burst water pipe. Look at the picture, and then write a paragraph explaining how you would attempt to fix this problem. Try to use the Word Power words in your paragraph.

WORD POWER

cautious: careful

concern: a reason to worry

unanticipated: not expected

A   What Is Process?

When you describe a **process**, you tell readers how something works or how to do something. For example, you could explain how the optical scanner at the checkout counter of a food store works or how to shorten a pair of jeans.

ASSIGNMENTS FOR PROCESS

You will use process in many of your college classes. Here are some typical assignments:

- *In a political science class:* Describe the process by which the United States Constitution is amended.

- *In a business course:* How should the owner of a small business go about making a business plan?

- *In a chemistry class:* Describe the Haber process for synthesizing ammonia.

A **process paragraph** presents a series of steps to explain how something works (or happens) or how to perform an action. A process paragraph contains the following elements:

- A process paragraph begins with a topic sentence that identifies the process. It should also state the main idea you want to make about this process.

- The topic sentence is followed by the steps in the process.

- These steps are presented one at a time, in strict **time order**—the order in which they occur or are to be performed.

- The paragraph ends with a concluding statement that brings the process to a close and sums up the paragraph's main idea.

Paragraph Map: Writing a Process Paragraph

Topic sentence _____

_____

Step #1 _____

_____

Step #2 _____

_____

Step #3 _____

_____

Concluding statement _____

_____

There are two types of process paragraphs: **process explanations** and **instructions**.

Process Explanations

In a **process explanation**, your purpose is to tell how something works or how something happens—for example, how a cell phone operates or how the body digests food. In this case, you do not expect readers to perform the process.

The following paragraph explains how a fire extinguisher works.

How a Fire Extinguisher Works

Even though many people have fire extinguishers in their homes, most people do not know how they work. A fire extinguisher is a metal cylinder filled with a substance that will put out a fire. All extinguishers operate the same way. First, the material inside the cylinder is put under pressure. Next, when a lever on top of the metal cylinder is squeezed, a valve is opened, and the pressure inside the fire extinguisher is released. As the compressed gas in the cylinder rushes out, it carries the material in the fire extinguisher along with it. Then, a nozzle at the top of the cylinder concentrates the stream of liquid, gas, or powder coming from the fire extinguisher so it can be aimed at a fire. Finally, the material comes in contact with the fire and puts it out. Every home should have at least one fire extinguisher located where it can be easily reached when it is needed. Most important, everyone should know how to use a fire extinguisher.

— David Turner (student)

Topic sentence

Transitions introduce steps in process

Concluding statement

Instructions

When you write **instructions**, your purpose is to give readers the information they need to perform a task or activity—for example, to fill out an application or to operate a piece of machinery. Because you expect readers to follow your instructions, you address them directly, using **commands** (*check the gauge . . . pull the valve*).

The following paragraph gives humorous instructions on how to get food out of a vending machine.

Man vs. Machine

Long ago, the first food machines were the servants of people. Now, these machines have turned against their creators. The result is a generation of machines that will take a little girl's allowance and keep her Cheetos, too. Luckily, there is a foolproof method for getting a vending machine to give

Topic sentence

Transitions introduce steps in process

Concluding statement

up its food. First, approach the vending machine coolly. Make sure that you don't seem frightened or angry. The machine will sense these emotions and steal your money. Second, be polite. Say hello, compliment the machine on its selection of goodies, and smile. Be careful. If the machine thinks you are trying to take advantage of it, it will keep your money. Third, if the machine steals your money, remain calm. Ask it nicely to give you the food you paid for. Finally, it is time to get serious. Hit the side of the vending machine with your fist. If this doesn't work, lower your shoulder, and throw yourself at the machine. (A good kick or two might also help.) When the machine has had enough, it will drop your snack, and you can grab it. If you follow these few simple steps, you should have no trouble walking away from vending machines with the food you paid for.

— Adam Cooper (student)

Transitions are important in process paragraphs. They enable readers to identify each step—for example, *first, second, third,* and so on. In addition, they establish a sequence that helps readers move easily through the process.

Some Transitional Words and Phrases for Process

after that	first	soon
as	immediately	the first (second, third) step
as soon as	later	the last step
at the same time	meanwhile	then
at this point	next	the next step
before	now	when
finally	once	while

GRAMMAR IN CONTEXT

Process

When you write a process paragraph, you may find yourself making **illogical shifts** in tense, person, number, and voice. If you shift from one tense, person, or voice to another without good reason, you may confuse readers.

CONFUSING First, the vending machine should be approached coolly. Make sure that you don't seem frightened or angry. (illogical shift from passive to active voice)

(continued on following page)

Process, continued from previous page

CLEAR First, approach the vending machine coolly. Make sure that you don't seem frightened or angry. (consistent use of active voice)

For information on how to avoid illogical shifts in tense, person, and voice, see Chapter 23.

B Writing a Process Paragraph

■ PRACTICE 8-1

Read this process paragraph, and answer the questions that follow it.

Getting a Tattoo

Before getting a tattoo, a customer should understand the process. First, the customer should find an experienced and responsible tattoo artist, one who has state certification. Also, the shop should be clean, and all equipment that is not disposable should be carefully sterilized. Next, the customer should work with the tattoo artist to select a design from the artist's portfolio. Later, while the customer sits in a chair, the artist will transfer a stencil of the design onto the skin. After this step, the artist will use an inked needle to create the tattoo. Once the tattoo is completed, the artist should apply ointment and a bandage to the affected area. Eventually, the tattoo will scab over and heal. Most customers find the process less painful than they had expected, and they are usually pleased with the results.

—Ryan Felder (student)

1. Underline the topic sentence of the paragraph.

2. List the transitions that tell you that the writer is moving on to another step in the process. The first transition has been listed for you.
   First

3. List the steps in the process on the lines below.

_____

_____

_____

_____

_____

_____

_____

4. Underline the paragraph's concluding statement.

STRATEGIES FOR COLLEGE SUCCESS

Prioritizing Tasks

If you are facing several important tasks—such as papers and exams in several classes—list them in order of decreasing importance. You may decide that tasks for your strongest subjects can wait while the subject you are in danger of failing needs immediate attention. For additional tips on how to become a successful student, see Chapter 1.

■ PRACTICE 8-2

Following are four topic sentences for process paragraphs. List three steps that might occur in each process.

1. Registering for college courses can be a frustrating process.

_____

_____

_____

2. Balancing a checkbook is not as complicated as it may seem.

_____

_____

_____

3. Driving on a snowy road is not difficult if you follow a few simple
    steps.

    _____

    _____

    _____

4. Buying products online can save you time and money.

    _____

    _____

    _____

PRACTICE 8-3

Choose one of the topics below (or a topic of your own) as the subject
of a process paragraph.

How to succeed in college	How to live with a roommate
Writing a letter of complaint	Studying for a test
Getting out of debt	How to quit smoking
Planning a party	Living on a budget
Deciding which gym to join	Dressing well
Succeeding at a job interview	Breaking up with someone
How to play your favorite	How to rent an apartment
board game	How to throw a curve ball

PRACTICE 8-4

Use one or more of the strategies described in 3C to help you come
up with as many steps as you can for the topic you have chosen. List
these steps on a separate sheet of paper.

PRACTICE 8-5

Review the steps you listed in Practice 8-4, and decide whether to
write a process explanation or a set of instructions. Then, choose the
steps you want to include from the list you made in Practice 8-4, and
list them below.

- _____   - _____

- _____   - _____

- _____   - _____

- _____   - _____

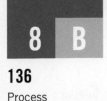

PRACTICE 8-6

Reread your list of steps from Practice 8-5. Then, draft a topic sentence that identifies the process you will discuss and communicates the point you will make about it.

Topic sentence: _____

_____

_____

PRACTICE 8-7

Review the steps you listed in Practice 8-5. Then, write them down in time order, moving from the first step to the last.

1. _____   5. _____

2. _____   6. _____

3. _____   7. _____

4. _____   8. _____

PRACTICE 8-8

Draft your process paragraph.

PRACTICE 8-9

Using the Self-Assessment Checklist on page 137, revise your process paragraph.

PRACTICE 8-10

Print out a final draft of your process paragraph.

✓ Seeing and Writing: Skills Check

Look back at your response to the Seeing and Writing activity on page 129. Reread it, and answer the following questions:

- Is your paragraph unified?
- Is your paragraph well developed?
- Is your paragraph coherent?

Then, revise and edit your paragraph.

✓ Self-Assessment Checklist

Writing a Process Paragraph

☐ Does the topic sentence identify the process your paragraph will discuss?

☐ Does the topic sentence indicate whether you are giving instructions or explaining how something works?

☐ Do you include all the steps in the process?

☐ Do you present the steps in the order in which they occur?

☐ Have you included the transitions that readers will need to follow the process?

☐ Have you avoided illogical shifts in tense, person, number, and voice?

☐ Have you included a concluding statement that sums up your paragraph's main idea?

CHAPTER REVIEW

1. The following student process paragraph is missing a topic sentence, transitional words and phrases, and a concluding statement. After reading the paragraph, fill in the missing elements on the appropriate lines below. (See p. 132 for a list of transitions.)

Starting Over

_____

_____

Before you begin dating, keep in mind that you should date only when you are ready. _____, once you decide to go out on a date, is to take things slowly. Both you and your children need to get used to the fact that you are dating. _____, make sure that your children are well cared for when you are on a date. Parents or close friends are best because your children will feel safe with them. _____, talk to your children. Explain that you would like to spend time with someone you like. Do not talk about marriage or getting them a "new parent." _____, if you decide you would like to introduce the person

you are dating to your children, keep the first visit short, and schedule additional visits far apart. Also, do not show your date too much affection in front of your children. _____, be patient. It may take a long time for both you and your children to become comfortable with your new life. _____

_____

2. Create a process paragraph by adding details to support the topic sentence below. Connect the steps in the process with appropriate transitions, and end the paragraph with a clear concluding statement that sums up the main idea. Finally, add an appropriate title on the line provided.

_____

Facebook and other social networking sites can be good places to meet new friends if you follow a few simple steps to protect your privacy. _____

_____

_____

_____

_____

_____

_____

_____

_____

_____

_____

_____

_____

_____

3. The picture below shows a waitress at work. Look carefully at the
    picture, and write a process paragraph in which you explain how to
    do a job you've held. Begin your paragraph with a topic sentence that
    identifies the process you are describing. Then, in the rest of the para-
    graph, present the steps of the process in clear chronological order.

Cause and Effect

SEEING AND WRITING ▲

The picture above shows a recent *Project Runway* winner. Look at the picture, and imagine how your life would change if you won this competition. Then, write a paragraph in which you discuss how winning *Project Runway* would affect you and the people you know. Try to use the Word Power words in your paragraph.

A — What Is Cause and Effect?

Why is the cost of college so high? How does smoking affect a person's health? How dangerous is swine flu? All these familiar questions have one thing in common: they try to determine the causes or effects of an action, event, or situation.

A **cause** is something or someone that makes something happen. An **effect** is something brought about by a particular cause.

Cause	Effect
Increased airport security ⟶	Long lines at airports
Weight gain ⟶	Decision to exercise
Seatbelt laws passed ⟶	Increased use of seatbelts

ASSIGNMENTS FOR CAUSE AND EFFECT

You will use cause and effect in many of your college classes. Here are some typical assignments:

- *In a history class:* What were the main causes of the Great Depression?
- *In a nutrition class:* Explain the nutritional effects of trans fats.
- *In a nursing course:* How will national health-care legislation affect the practice of nursing?

A **cause-and-effect paragraph** helps readers understand why something happened or is happening or shows readers how one event or situation affects something else. A cause-and-effect paragraph contains the following elements:

- A **cause-and-effect paragraph** begins with a topic sentence that states the paragraph's main idea; it tells readers whether the paragraph is focusing on causes or on effects.

- The topic sentence is followed by the causes or the effects, one at a time.

- The causes or effects are arranged in **logical order**—for example, from least important to most important.

- The paragraph ends with a concluding statement that sums up its main idea.

Paragraph Map: Writing a Cause-and-Effect Paragraph

Topic sentence _____

_____

Cause (or effect) #1 _____

_____

Cause (or effect) #2 _____

_____

Cause (or effect) #3 _____

_____

Concluding statement _____

_____

The following paragraph focuses on causes.

Health Alert

Topic sentence

For a number of reasons, Americans are gaining weight at an alarming rate. First, many Americans do not eat healthy foods. Instead, they eat a lot of food that is high in salt and contains a lot of saturated fat. Also, many Americans eat on the run, grabbing a doughnut or muffin on the way to work

Transitions introduce causes of weight gain

and eating fast food for lunch or dinner. Another reason Americans are gaining weight is that they eat too much. They take too much food and think they must eat everything on their plates. They do not stop eating when they are full, and they often have second helpings and dessert. The most important reason for this alarming weight gain is that Americans do not exercise. They sit on the couch and watch hours of television and get up only to have a snack or a soda.

Concluding statement

The effect of this unhealthy lifestyle is easy to predict. Unless Americans begin eating better, many will develop severe health problems in the future.

— Jen Toll (student)

The paragraph below focuses on effects.

Second Thoughts

Topic sentence

When I dropped out of high school before my senior year, I had no idea how this action would affect my life. The first effect was that I became a social outcast. At the beginning, my friends called and asked me to go out with them. Gradually, however, school activities took up more and more of their time. Eventually, they had no time for me. Another effect was that I became stuck in a dead-end job. When I was in school, working part time at a bookstore didn't seem bad. Once it became my full-time job, however, I saw that I was going nowhere, but without a diploma or some college education, I couldn't get a better job. The most important effect was that my girlfriend broke up with me. One day she told me that she didn't like dating a dropout. She said I had no goals and no future. I had to agree with her. When I heard that she had started dating a sophomore in college, something clicked. I enrolled in night school and got my GED, and then I applied to community college. Now that I am taking college classes, I realize how wrong I was to drop out of high school and how lucky I am to have a second chance.

— Dan Tarr (student)

> **Transitions introduce
> effects of dropping out**

> **Concluding statement**

Transitions in cause-and-effect paragraphs show the connections between a cause and its effects or between an effect and its causes. In addition, they identify the relationship between various causes or effects—for example, which cause or effect is more important than another or which comes before another.

Some Transitional Words and Phrases for Cause and Effect

another cause	moreover	the first (second, third, final) reason
another effect	one cause	
as a result	(effect, reason)	the most important cause
because	since	the most important effect
besides	so	
consequently	the first (second, third, final) cause	the most important reason
finally		therefore
for	the first (second, third, final) effect	
for this reason		

> ## GRAMMAR IN CONTEXT
> ### Cause and Effect
>
> When you write a cause-and-effect paragraph, be careful not to confuse the words *affect* and *effect*. *Affect* is a verb meaning "to influence." *Effect* is a noun meaning "result."
>
> *effect*
> The first ~~affect~~ is that I became a social outcast. (*effect*
>
> is a noun)
>
> When I dropped out of high school before my senior year, I
> *affect*
> had no idea how this action would ~~effect~~ my life. (*affect* is a
>
> verb)
>
> For more information on *effect* and *affect*, see Chapter 36.

B Writing a Cause-and-Effect Paragraph

■ PRACTICE 9-1

Read this cause-and-effect paragraph, and answer the questions that follow it.

Why I Had to Move

It's hard to imagine why someone would go to all the trouble and expense of moving, but I had some very good reasons for moving to a new apartment. My first reason for moving was that I had noisy neighbors. When I looked at the apartment, the rental agent promised me that it would be quiet. He didn't bother to tell me that the apartment across the hall was rented by two guys who came and went at all hours of the day and night. Every weekend, and most nights, they had friends over, and this made it impossible for me to sleep or to study. Another reason that I moved was that the landlord never fixed things. The stove never worked right, and I could never be sure if I would have heat or hot water. My most disturbing reason for moving was that the landlord made a habit of coming into my apartment without telling me. As soon as I moved in, I began to notice that something wasn't right. I would come home from classes and notice that the door wasn't locked—even though I remembered locking it. Once I noticed that my DVD player had been disconnected and that a drawer that I had closed was open. Later, a neighbor told me that the landlord came around and inspected all the apartments once a month.

When I told the rental agent that the landlord shouldn't come into my apartment anytime he felt like it, he told me to read my lease. By the end of the year, I decided that I had had enough, and I moved.

— Jenny Wong (student)

1. Underline the topic sentence of the paragraph.

2. Does the paragraph focus on causes or effects? How do you know?

_____

_____

_____

3. List the transitions that tell you the writer is moving from one cause to another.

_____

_____

_____

4. List the causes on the lines below.

_____

_____

_____

5. Underline the paragraph's concluding statement.

STRATEGIES FOR COLLEGE SUCCESS
Customizing Your Study Schedule

Identify the times of day when you feel most alert. Also notice which study locations work best for you. Do you get the most done in the early morning in a quiet library or late at night in a busy coffee shop? Use this information to help you customize your schedule. For additional tips on how to become a successful student, see Chapter 1.

PRACTICE 9-2

Following are four topic sentences for cause-and-effect paragraphs. List three causes or effects for each sentence.

1. Indoor air pollution is caused by products we use every day.

_____

_____

2. Second-hand smoke can have harmful effects on everyone's health.

_____

_____

3. MP3 players are popular for many reasons.

_____

_____

4. Cell phones have changed our society.

_____

_____

PRACTICE 9-3

Choose one of the topics below (or a topic of your own) as the subject of a cause-and-effect paragraph.

Causes of problems falling asleep

Effects of lack of communication on a relationship

Causes of road rage

Effects of social networking sites

Why you attend the college you do

Effects of excessive drinking

Causes of binge drinking among young adults

The possible effects of climate change

Why people shop online

Why you belong to a particular organization

Effects of divorce on children

Why certain students succeed

Why print newspapers are dying

The reasons students cheat

Causes of low voter turnout

Why fast-food restaurants are so popular

The effects of peer pressure

PRACTICE 9-4

Freewrite or brainstorm to help you think of as many causes or effects as you can for the topic you have chosen.

PRACTICE 9-5

Review your notes for Practice 9-4, and create a cluster diagram. Write the topic in the center of the page, and draw arrows branching out to specific causes or effects.

PRACTICE 9-6

Choose the most important causes or effects from your notes for Practices 9-4 and 9-5. List them on the lines that follow.

- _____
- _____
- _____
- _____
- _____
- _____

PRACTICE 9-7

Reread your list of causes or effects from Practice 9-6. Then, draft a topic sentence that introduces your topic and communicates the point you want to make about it.

Topic sentence: _____

_____

_____

PRACTICE 9-8

List the causes or effects you will discuss in your paragraph, arranging them in an effective order—for example, from least important to most important.

1. _____

2. _____

3. _____

4. _____

5. _____

6. _____

PRACTICE 9-9

Draft your cause-and-effect paragraph.

PRACTICE 9-10

Using the Self-Assessment Checklist on page 148, revise your cause-and-effect paragraph.

PRACTICE 9-11

Print out a final draft of your cause-and-effect paragraph.

✓ **Seeing and Writing: Skills Check**

Look back at your response to the Seeing and Writing activity on page 140. Reread it, and answer the following questions:

- Is your paragraph unified?
- Is your paragraph well developed?
- Is your paragraph coherent?

Then, revise and edit your paragraph.

✓ **Self-Assessment Checklist**

Writing a Cause-and-Effect Paragraph

☐ Does your topic sentence clearly state your paragraph's main idea?

☐ Does the topic sentence indicate whether the focus of the paragraph is on causes or on effects?

☐ Are the causes and effects clearly identified?

☐ Do transitional words and phrases signal a shift from one cause or effect to another?

☐ Have you used *affect* and *effect* correctly?

☐ Have you included a concluding statement that sums up your paragraph's main idea?

CHAPTER REVIEW

1. The following student cause-and-effect paragraph is missing a topic sentence, transitional words and phrases, and a concluding statement. After reading the paragraph, fill in the missing elements on the appropriate lines below. (See p. 143 for a list of transitions.)

Doing My Part

_____

_____

_____ is that I recycle. I try to separate bottles, cans, and paper. I

even recycle used cooking oil and old batteries that I replaced. Our township requires us to separate trash, but many people just put everything into a big plastic bag and throw it away. I choose to recycle. _____ is that I take public transportation when I commute to school. That way, I use less gas and oil. If more people took the train, we would all help to cut down on the pollution in the world. Besides, when I leave my car at home, I save money. I don't have to pay for gas, parking, or bridge tolls. _____ is that I buy items that can be reused before they are thrown away. For example, instead of using paper towels, I use cloth hand towels that I wash. I even refill the empty ink cartridges from my printer so that I can use them again. _____

_____

2. Create a cause-and-effect paragraph by adding causes to support the topic sentence below. Connect the effects with appropriate transitions, and end the paragraph with a clear concluding statement that sums up the main idea. Finally, add an appropriate title on the line provided.

_____

A number of factors can cause students to do poorly on exams.

_____
_____
_____
_____
_____
_____
_____
_____
_____
_____
_____
_____

3. The picture below shows a scene from the video game *Mortal Kombat*. Look carefully at the picture, and write a cause-and-effect paragraph that tells how violent video games affect the people who play them. Do you think they are dangerous, or do you think they are just harmless entertainment? Begin with a topic sentence that states the main idea of your paragraph. In the rest of the paragraph, discuss the effects that are relevant to your topic sentence.

Comparison and Contrast

CHAPTER 10

PREVIEW

In this chapter, you will learn to write a comparison-and-contrast paragraph.

SEEING AND WRITING ▲

The picture above shows a big dog and a little dog. Look at the picture, and then write a paragraph in which you compare these two dogs. Tell how they are alike, and then tell how they are different. Try to use the Word Power words in your paragraph.

WORD POWER
affectionate: loving
ferocious: fierce
intimidating: threatening
timid: shy, nervous

What Is Comparison and Contrast?

When you **compare**, you consider how two things are similar. When you **contrast**, you consider how they are different.

ASSIGNMENTS FOR COMPARISON AND CONTRAST

You will use comparison and contrast in many of your college classes. Here are some typical assignments:

- *In an information technology course:* Assume that the company for which you are working is considering changing from PCs to Macs. Write a report in which you compare the two types of computers.
- *In a literature course:* Compare the main characters in the plays *Death of a Salesman* by Arthur Miller and *Fences* by August Wilson.
- *In a world religions class:* Contrast the doctrines of sin and redemption in Christianity and Islam.

Comparison-and-contrast paragraphs can examine just similarities or just differences, or they can examine both. A comparison-and-contrast paragraph contains the following elements:

- A comparison-and-contrast paragraph begins with a topic sentence that states its main idea and tells readers whether the paragraph is going to discuss similarities or differences.
- The topic sentence is followed by a discussion of the same or similar points for both subjects.
- Points should be arranged in **logical order**—for example, from least important to most important.
- The paragraph ends with a concluding statement that sums up the main idea.

There are two kinds of comparison-and-contrast paragraphs—*subject-by-subject comparisons* and *point-by-point comparisons*.

Subject-by-Subject Comparisons

In a **subject-by-subject comparison**, you divide your comparison into two parts and discuss one subject at a time. In the first part of the paragraph, you discuss all your points about one subject. Then, in the second part, you discuss all your points about the other subject.

A subject-by-subject comparison is best for short paragraphs in which you do not discuss too many points. Readers will have little difficulty remembering the points you discuss for your first subject as you move on to discuss the second subject.

Paragraph Map: Writing a Subject-by-Subject Comparison Paragraph

Topic sentence _____

_____

Subject A _____
Point 1 _____

_____

Point 2 _____

_____

Point 3 _____

_____

Subject B _____
Point 1 _____

_____

Point 2 _____

_____

Point 3 _____

_____

Concluding statement _____

_____

The following paragraph uses a subject-by-subject comparison to compare two ways of telling time.

Why I Wear a Watch

Cell phones may be the modern way to check the time, but I prefer a good, old-fashioned watch. A watch is always right there when I need it, allowing me to do a quick time check. Also, watches let me show my style. My sleek chrome watch helps me look professional when I am at work, and my retro-style digital watch lets me show a funkier side at school or on the weekends. In addition, watches can have sentimental value. My chrome watch was a high-school graduation gift from my grandmother, and I bought the digital watch while on a road trip with my best friend. Cell phones also tell time, but they are not as practical or as much fun as watches. Compared to my watches, my cell phone is often hard to find when I'm out. Sometimes I have to stop on the street or in a busy train station and dig around in my backpack for it. Also, unlike watches, cell phones do not let me show my style. Of course, I can get different covers for my phone, but I cannot change

Topic sentence

Subject A: My watches

Transitions emphasize differences

Subject B: My cell phone

its shape. Finally, I cannot imagine forming a sentimental attachment to a
phone. My watches remind me of people and important occasions, but my cell
phone has no special memories associated with it. As long as my watches keep
ticking, I will save my cell phone for talking and texting.

— Tonya Jones (student)

Point-by-Point Comparisons

In a **point-by-point comparison**, you discuss a point about one subject
and then discuss the same point about the second subject. You use this
alternating pattern throughout the paragraph.

A point-by-point comparison is a good strategy for paragraphs in
which you discuss many points. It is also a good choice if the points you
are discussing are technical or complicated.

Paragraph Map: Writing a Point-by-Point Comparison Paragraph

Topic sentence _____

_____

Point 1 _____

Subject A _____

_____

Subject B _____

_____

Point 2 _____

Subject A _____

_____

Subject B _____

_____

Point 3 _____

Subject A _____

_____

Subject B _____

_____

Concluding statement _____

_____

The following paragraph uses a point-by-point comparison to compare two characters in a short story.

Two Sisters

Although they grew up together, Maggie and Dee, the two sisters in Alice Walker's short story "Everyday Use," are very different. Maggie, who was burned in a fire, is shy and has low self-esteem. When she walks, she shuffles her feet and looks down at the ground. Dee, however, is confident and outgoing. She looks people in the eye when she talks to them and is very opinionated. Maggie seems satisfied with her life. She never complains or asks for anything more than she has, and she has remained at home with her mother in rural Georgia. In contrast, Dee has always wanted nicer things. She has gone away to school and hardly ever visits her mother and Maggie. The biggest difference between Maggie and Dee is their attitude toward tradition. Although Maggie values her family's traditions, Dee values her African roots. Maggie cherishes her family's handmade quilts and furniture, hoping to use them with her own family. Unlike Maggie, Dee sees the handmade objects as things to be displayed, not used. The many differences between Maggie and Dee add conflict and tension to the story.

— Margaret Caracappa (student)

Topic sentence

— Point 1: Different personalities

— Point 2: Different attitudes toward life

— Point 3: Different attitudes toward tradition

Transitions emphasize differences between two subjects

Concluding statement

Transitions are important in a comparison-and-contrast paragraph. Transitions tell readers when you are moving from one point (or one subject) to another. Transitions also show readers whether you are focusing on similarities (for example, *likewise* or *similarly*) or on differences (for example, *although* or *in contrast*).

Some Transitional Words and Phrases for Comparison and Contrast

although	nevertheless
but	one difference . . . another difference
compared to	one similarity . . . another similarity
even though	on the contrary
however	on the one hand . . . on the other hand
in comparison	similarly
in contrast	though
like	unlike
likewise	whereas

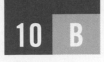

GRAMMAR IN CONTEXT

Comparison and Contrast

When you write a comparison-and-contrast paragraph, you should state the points you are comparing in **parallel** terms—using the same patterns of words to expresss similarities or differences.

NOT PARALLEL   Although Maggie values her family's traditions, the African heritage of their family is the thing that Dee values.

PARALLEL   Although Maggie values her family's traditions, Dee values their African roots.

For more information on revising to make ideas parallel, see Chapter 19.

B   Writing a Comparison-and-Contrast Paragraph

PRACTICE 10-1

Read this comparison-and-contrast paragraph, and answer the questions that follow it.

Life after Smoking

Having been both a smoker and a nonsmoker, I believe I am qualified to compare the two ways of life. When I smoked, I often found myself banished from public places such as offices, restaurants, and stores when I felt the urge to smoke. I would huddle with my fellow smokers outside, in all kinds of weather, just for a cigarette. As more and more people stopped smoking, I found myself banished from private homes, too. I spent a lot of money on cigarettes, and the prices seemed to rise faster and faster. I worried about lung cancer and heart disease. My colds wouldn't go away, and they often turned into bronchitis. Climbing stairs and running left me breathless. Now that I have stopped smoking, my life is different. I can go anywhere and socialize with anyone. The money I have saved in the last year on cigarettes is going to pay for a winter vacation in Florida. After not smoking for only a few weeks, I could breathe more easily, and I had more energy for running and climbing stairs. I have also avoided colds so far, and I'm not as worried about lung and heart disease. In fact, I've been told that my lungs should be as healthy as those of a nonsmoker within another year or so. All in all, quitting smoking was one of the smartest moves I ever made.

— Margaret Gonzales (student)

WORD POWER

banished: sent away from a place as punishment

10 B

157

Writing a
Comparison-
and-Contrast
Paragraph

1. Underline the topic sentence of the paragraph.

2. Does this paragraph deal mainly with similarities or differences?

   _____

   How do you know?

   _____

   _____

3. Is this paragraph a subject-by-subject or a point-by-point comparison?
   How do you know?

   _____

   _____

   _____

   _____

4. List some of the contrasts the writer describes. The first contrast has
   been listed for you.

   When she was a smoker, she often had to smoke outside of public and

   private places. As a nonsmoker, she can go anywhere.

   _____

   _____

   _____

   _____

   _____

5. Underline the paragraph's concluding statement.

STRATEGIES FOR COLLEGE SUCCESS
Doing Homework in a Group

You may want to try doing homework with a group of your classmates. Everyone will benefit from the chance to share information,
and you may learn new approaches to doing assignments. For additional tips on how to become a successful student, see Chapter 1.

▇ PRACTICE 10-2 ▇

Following are four topic sentences for comparison-and-contrast paragraphs. First, identify the two things being compared. Then, list three
similarities or differences between the two subjects. For example, if
you were comparing two authors, you could show the similarities and/
or differences in the subjects they write about, in their styles of writing, and in the kinds of readers they attract.

1. All things considered, I would rather be happy than rich.

   _____

   _____

   _____

2. The media's portrayal of young people is often very negative, but the true picture is more positive.

   _____

   _____

   _____

3. Two styles of music that I like are very similar.

   _____

   _____

   _____

4. As soon as I arrive at work, I become a different person.

   _____

   _____

   _____

■ PRACTICE 10-3

Choose one of the following topics (or a topic of your own) as the subject of a comparison-and-contrast paragraph.

Two different TV news shows
The differences between two
   political candidates
What you thought college
   would be like before you
   started and what it actually
   is like
Two different sports
How people see you and how
   you really are
A book and a movie based
   on the book
Two different electronic devices
How you and your best friend
   are alike (or different)
Two different movie stars

Online classes and traditional
   classes
Two different views of your
   parents—how you saw them
   when you were a child and
   how you see them now
Technology today and ten
   years ago
Differences in the lives of the
   rich and poor
Two different careers
Two different late-night hosts
Small-town life versus big-city
   life
Two different bosses or
   teachers

10 B

159

Writing a
Comparison-
and-Contrast
Paragraph

PRACTICE 10-4

Use one or more of the strategies described in 3C to help you think of
as many similarities or differences as you can for the topic you have
chosen. (If you use clustering, create a separate cluster diagram for
each of the two subjects you are comparing.)

PRACTICE 10-5

Review your notes on the topic you chose in Practice 10-3. Decide
whether to focus on similarities or differences. On the following lines, list the similarities or differences that can best help you
develop a comparison-and-contrast paragraph on the topic you have
chosen.

_____

_____

_____

PRACTICE 10-6

Reread your list of similarities or differences from Practice 10-5.
Then, draft a topic sentence that introduces your two subjects and
indicates whether your paragraph will focus on similarities
or differences.

Topic sentence: _____

_____

_____

PRACTICE 10-7

Decide whether you will write a subject-by-subject or a point-by-point
comparison. Then, use the appropriate outline below to help you plan
your paragraph. Before you begin, decide on the order in which you
will present your points—for example, from least important to most
important. (For a subject-by-subject paragraph, begin by deciding
which subject you will discuss first.)

Subject-by-Subject Comparison

Subject A _____

   Point 1 _____

   Point 2 _____

   Point 3 _____

Subject B _____

    Point 1 _____

    Point 2 _____

    Point 3 _____

Point-by-Point Comparison

Point 1 _____

    Subject A _____

    Subject B _____

Point 2 _____

    Subject A _____

    Subject B _____

Point 3 _____

    Subject A _____

    Subject B _____

PRACTICE 10-8

Draft your comparison-and-contrast paragraph.

PRACTICE 10-9

Using the Self-Assessment Checklist on page 161, revise your comparison-and-contrast paragraph.

PRACTICE 10-10

Print out a final draft of your comparison-and-contrast paragraph.

> ### ✓ Seeing and Writing: Skills Check
>
> Look back at your response to the Seeing and Writing activity on page 151. Reread it, and answer the following questions:
>
> - Is your paragraph unified?
> - Is your paragraph well developed?
> - Is your paragraph coherent?
>
> Then, revise and edit your paragraph.

✓ **Self-Assessment Checklist**

Writing a Comparison-and-Contrast Paragraph

☐ Does your topic sentence state your paragraph's main idea?

☐ Does your topic sentence indicate the two things you will compare?

☐ Have you followed the correct format for a subject-by-subject or a point-by-point comparison?

☐ Have you discussed the same or similar points for both subjects?

☐ Have you used appropriate transitional words and phrases?

☐ Have you stated your points in parallel terms?

☐ Have you included a concluding statement that sums up your paragraph's main idea?

CHAPTER REVIEW

1. The following student comparison-and-contrast paragraph is missing a topic sentence, transitional words and phrases, and a concluding statement. After reading the paragraph, fill in the missing elements on the appropriate lines below. (See p. 155 for a list of transitions.)

Farmers' Markets and Supermarkets

_____

_____ _____ to

supermarket produce, locally grown food comes in many unusual varieties.

In the fall, for instance, my town's farmers' market is loaded with different

varieties of apples, such as Autumn Gold, Cherry Pippin, and Eddie April.

_____the owners of large factory farms that supply supermarket chains,

local farmers are willing to invest the time and energy in growing unusual

varieties of fruits and vegetables. Also, _____ the produce at

supermarkets, the local food at my farmers' market is always very fresh because

it has been transported only a few miles. The produce in the supermarket,

_____, may have been transported across the country or around the world. To me, the biggest advantage of buying locally grown food is the social atmosphere at my farmers' market. _____I want to get in and out of the supermarket as fast as possible, I like to spend time at the farmers' market. I enjoy talking to the farmers and meeting other people who are interested in locally grown food. Also, the farmers' market often features bands, cooking demonstrations, and other entertainment, so it's often hard to leave.

_____

2. Create a comparison-and-contrast paragraph by adding points that support the topic sentence below, contrasting your goals in high school and your goals today. Connect the points with appropriate transitions, and end the paragraph with a clear concluding statement that sums up the main idea. Finally, add an appropriate title on the line provided.

_____

When I was in high school, my goals were different from what they are today. _____

_____

_____

_____

_____

_____

_____

_____

_____

_____

_____

_____

_____

_____

3. Both of the pictures below show boxers. Look carefully at the two pictures, and write a paragraph in which you compare them. Begin with a topic sentence that states the main idea of your paragraph. Then, in the rest of the paragraph, discuss the points that support the topic sentence. End your paragraph with a concluding statement that sums up your paragraph's main idea.

"Rocky" statue, Philadelphia, PA (left); professional boxer, after winning a fight (right).

Classification

PREVIEW

In this chapter, you will learn to write a classification paragraph.

SEEING AND WRITING ▲

The picture above shows a small neighborhood store. Look at the picture, and then write a paragraph discussing several kinds of stores in your neighborhood. For example, you could discuss mom-and-pop stores (such as bodegas), convenience stores (such as 7-Elevens), and superstores (such as Walmart). Try to use the Word Power words in your paragraph.

A   What Is Classification?

Classification is the act of sorting items (people, things, or ideas) into categories. You classify when you organize your bills into those you have to pay now and those you can pay later. You also classify when you sort the clothes in a dresser drawer into piles of socks, T-shirts, and underwear.

ASSIGNMENTS FOR CLASSIFICATION

You will use classification in many of your college classes. Here are some typical assignments:

- *In a history class:* Classify (and discuss) the various groups that fought in the American Revolution.
- *In a sociology course:* Write an essay in which you classify the people you meet according to the roles they play in society.
- *In a management class:* Evaluate several businesses in your area—for example, supermarkets or pharmacies—according to the types and quality of the products or services they provide.

In a **classification paragraph**, you tell readers how items can be sorted into categories or groups. A classification paragraph contains the following elements:

- The topic sentence states the main idea of the paragraph (and often identifies the categories you will discuss).

- The topic sentence is followed by a discussion of each of the categories, one at a time. Your discussion of each category should include enough details and examples to show how it is different from the other categories.

- The categories are arranged in **logical order**—for example, from most important to least important or from smallest to largest. Finally, each category should be distinct. In other words, none of the items in one category should also fit into another category.

- The paragraph ends with a concluding statement that sums up its main idea.

Paragraph Map: Writing a Classification Paragraph

Topic sentence _____

_____

Category #1 _____

_____

Category #2 _____

_____

Category #3 _____

_____

Concluding statement _____

_____

The writer of the following paragraph classifies items into three distinct groups.

Types of Bosses

Topic sentence

I've had three kinds of bosses in my life — the uninterested boss, the interested supervisor, and the over-interested micromanager. The first type is the uninterested boss. This boss doesn't care what workers do as long as they leave him alone. When I was a counselor at summer camp, my boss fell into this category. As long as no campers (or, worse yet, parents) complained, he left you alone. He never cared if you followed the activity

Transitions introduce three categories of bosses

plan for the day or gave the kids an extra snack to keep them quiet. The second type of boss is the helpful supervisor. This kind of boss will check you periodically and give you advice. You'll have a certain amount of freedom but not too much. When I was a salesperson at the Gap, my boss fell into this category. She helped me through the first few weeks of the job and encouraged me to do my best. By the end of the summer, I had learned a lot about the retail business and had good feelings about the job. The last, and worst, type of boss is the micromanager. This kind of boss gets involved in everything. My boss at Taco Bell was this kind of person. No one could do anything right. There was always a better way. If you rolled a burrito one way, he would tell you to do it another way. If you did it the other way, he would tell you to do it the first way. Because of the constant criticism, people quit all the time. This boss never seemed to understand that people need praise every once in a while. Even though the second type of boss — the supervisor — expects a lot and makes you work, it is clear to me that this boss is better than the other types.

Concluding statement

— Melissa Burrell (student)

Transitions are important in classification paragraphs. They introduce each new category and tell readers when you are moving from one category to another (for example, *the first type, the second type*). They can also indicate which categories you think are more important than others (for example, *the most important, the least important*)

Some Transitional Phrases for Classification

one kind . . . another kind	the first type . . . the second type
one way . . . another way	
the first (second, third) category	the most (or least) important group
the first group . . . the last group	

GRAMMAR IN CONTEXT
Classification

When you write a classification paragraph, you often list the categories you are going to discuss. If you use a colon to introduce your list, make sure that a complete sentence comes before the colon.

INCORRECT   Basically, bosses can be divided into: the uninterested boss, the supervisor, and the micromanager.

CORRECT   Basically, I've had three kinds of bosses in my life: the uninterested boss, the supervisor, and the micromanager.

For more information on how to use a colon to introduce a list, see 33B.

B Writing a Classification Paragraph

▮ PRACTICE 11-1

Read the classification paragraph below, and answer the questions that follow.

International Symbols

    Because many people travel to different countries, international symbols have been created to help them find what they need when they don't know the language. These symbols substitute for words. One group of symbols is for transportation. For example, airports post easy-to-understand pictures of planes, taxis, buses, and trains to help people get where they need to go. Another group of symbols is for travelers' personal needs. For example, men's and women's toilets have different symbols. There are signs for drinking fountains and baby-changing tables. A final group of symbols helps travelers when they get to their destinations. For example, international travelers often have to change their money in a new country. They can find a currency exchange at a sign that shows an American dollar, a British pound, and a Japanese yen. If they need to find a hotel or a restaurant, they can look for the sign with a bed or a knife and fork. Clearly, these symbols make it easier for people to travel in countries where they do not speak the language.

                                         — Laurent Fischer (student)

1. Underline the paragraph's topic sentence.

2. List the categories that the writer uses to classify the types of international symbols discussed.

    _____

    _____

    _____

3. List the transitional words and phrases that let the reader know that a new category is being introduced.

    _____

    _____

    _____

4. Underline the paragraph's concluding statement.

Keeping Track of Announcements

During a lecture, your instructor may make announcements. For example, he or she may announce quiz or exam dates or remind students to schedule conferences during the upcoming week. Copy this time-sensitive information into your calendar or organizer as soon as possible after class. For additional tips on how to become a successful student, see Chapter 1.

PRACTICE 11-2

Following are four topic sentences for classification paragraphs. For each sentence, list three or four categories under which information could be discussed.

1. On every road in the United States, motorists encounter three types of drivers.

2. Students can be sorted into a number of distinct categories.

3. Advertisers try to appeal to women in various ways.

4. Reality shows fall into several categories.

PRACTICE 11-3

Choose one of the topics below (or a topic of your own) as the subject of a classification paragraph.

Types of exercises   Parenting styles
Kinds of friends   Ways to relieve stress
Types of video games   Methods of arguing
Snack foods   Types of college pressures
Types of parties you've gone to   Types of sports fans
Kinds of part-time jobs   Kinds of teachers
Types of drivers   College courses
Popular music   Types of shoppers

PRACTICE 11-4

Use one or more of the strategies described in 3C to help you decide how to classify items for the topic you have chosen. Identify as many categories as you can.

PRACTICE 11-5

Review the list of categories you came up with for the topic you chose in Practice 11-3. On the following lines, list the three or four categories you can best develop in your paragraph.

Category 1 _____

Category 2 _____

Category 3 _____

Category 4 _____

PRACTICE 11-6

On the lines below and on the next page, list as many examples as you can for each category you chose in Practice 11-5.

Category 1 _____

    Example 1 _____

    Example 2 _____

    Example 3 _____

    Example 4 _____

Category 2 _____

    Example 1 _____

    Example 2 _____

    Example 3 _____

    Example 4 _____

Category 3 _____

    Example 1 _____

Example 2 _____

Example 3 _____

Example 4 _____

Category 4 _____

Example 1 _____

Example 2 _____

Example 3 _____

Example 4 _____

▮ PRACTICE 11-7

On the lines below, list the categories in the order in which you will discuss them.

Category 1 _____

Category 2 _____

Category 3 _____

Category 4 _____

▮ PRACTICE 11-8

Reread the list you made in Practice 11-6. Then, draft a topic sentence that states your main idea (and perhaps introduces the categories you will discuss).

Topic sentence: _____

_____

▮ PRACTICE 11-9

Draft your classification paragraph.

▮ PRACTICE 11-10

Using the Self-Assessment Checklist on page 172, revise your classification paragraph.

▮ PRACTICE 11-11

Print out a final draft of your classification paragraph.

✓ Seeing and Writing: Skills Check

Look back at your response to the Seeing and Writing activity on page 164. Reread it, and answer the following questions:

- Is your paragraph unified?
- Is your paragraph well developed?
- Is your paragraph coherent?

Then, revise and edit your paragraph.

✓ Self-Assessment Checklist

Writing a Classification Paragraph

☐ Does your topic sentence state your paragraph's main idea?

☐ Does your topic sentence introduce the categories you will discuss?

☐ Do you clearly identify each category and distinguish it from the others?

☐ Are the categories distinct from one another?

☐ Do you include enough examples in each category?

☐ Do transitional words and phrases signal the shift from one category to another?

☐ If you introduce your categories with a colon, do you have a complete sentence before the colon?

☐ Have you included a concluding statement that sums up your paragraph's main idea?

CHAPTER REVIEW

1. The following student classification paragraph is missing a topic sentence, transitional words and phrases, and a concluding statement. After reading the paragraph, fill in the missing elements on the appropriate lines below. (See p. 167 for a list of transitions.)

Types of Rocks

_____

_____

_____, igneous rock, is molten rock that has cooled and solidified. Igneous rocks, such as pumice and granite, are formed when volcanic eruptions bring molten rock to the earth's surface. Other types of igneous rocks are formed when molten rock solidifies slowly underground. _____, sedimentary rock, is formed from the sediment that is deposited at the bottom of the ocean. Sedimentary rocks, such as sandstone and shale, are deposited in layers, with the oldest sediments on the bottom and the newest on top. _____, metamorphic rock, is created by heat and pressure. These rocks are buried deep below the earth's surface for millions of years. The weight and high temperatures that they are exposed to change their structure and mineral composition. The most common metamorphic rocks are marble, slate, gneiss, and quartzite. _____

_____

_____

2. Create a classification paragraph by adding information about the three categories to support the topic sentence below. Make sure you connect the categories with appropriate transitions, and end the paragraph with a clear concluding statement that sums up the main idea. Finally, add an appropriate title on the line provided.

_____

There are three kinds of friends—those who are useful, those who are fun to be with, and those who make us better people. _____

_____

_____

_____

_____

_____

_____

_____

_____

3. The pictures below depict scenes from movies about teachers. Look carefully at the pictures, and write a paragraph that classifies the different types of teachers that you have encountered. Begin your paragraph with a topic sentence that states your main idea and introduces the categories you will discuss. Then, in the rest of the paragraph, discuss one kind of teacher at a time, presenting examples that show how each category is different from the others. End your paragraph with a concluding statement that sums up its main idea.

Ben Stein in Ferris Bueller

Morgan Freeman in Lean on Me

Michelle Pfeiffer in Dangerous Minds

Definition

CHAPTER 12

PREVIEW

- In this chapter, you will learn to write a definition paragraph.

SEEING AND WRITING ▲

The picture above shows firefighters leaving the rescue area near the World Trade Center after their shift on September 13, 2001. Look at the picture, and then write a paragraph in which you define the term *hero*. What qualities do you think heroes should possess? What people do you consider to be heroes? Try to use the Word Power words in your paragraph.

WORD POWER
courageous: brave
determined: firm, strong-minded
daring: bold
invincible: unbeatable

175

A What Is Definition?

During a conversation, you might say that a friend is *stubborn*, that a stream is *polluted*, or that a neighborhood is *dangerous*. To make yourself clear, you have to define what you mean by *stubborn*, *polluted*, or *dangerous*.

A **definition** tells what a word means. When you want your readers to know exactly how you are using a specific term, you define it.

When most people think of definitions, they think of the **formal definitions** they see in a dictionary. Formal definitions have a three-part structure that includes the following parts:

- The term to be defined
- The general class to which the term belongs
- The things that make the term different from all other items in the general class to which the term belongs

Term	Class	Differentiation
Ice hockey	is a game	played on ice by two teams on skates who use curved sticks to try to hit a puck into an opponent's goal.
Spaghetti	is a pasta	made in the shape of long, thin strings, usually served with a sauce.

A single-sentence formal definition is often not enough to define a specialized term (*point of view* or *premeditation*, for example), an abstract concept (*happiness* or *success*, for example), or a complicated subject (climate change, for example). In these cases, you may need to write a definition paragraph.

ASSIGNMENTS FOR DEFINITION

You will use definition in many of your college classes. The following assignments call for definition:

- *In a public health class:* What is *alternative medicine*?
- *In an American literature class:* Define *naturalism* as it is used in Richard Wright's novel *Native Son*.
- *In a course on constitutional law:* Is the death penalty "cruel and unusual punishment"?

A **definition paragraph** is an expanded formal definition. It develops the basic formal definition by giving more details and examples. A definition paragraph contains the following elements:

- A definition paragraph begins with a topic sentence that states the main idea, often including a formal definition.

- Definition paragraphs do not follow any one particular pattern of development. In fact, a definition paragraph may define a term by using any of the patterns discussed in this text. For example, a definition paragraph may explain a concept by *comparing* it to something else or by explaining a *process*.

- A definition paragraph ends with a concluding statement that sums up its main idea.

Here is one possible structure for a definition paragraph. Notice that it uses a combination of **narration** and **exemplification**.

Paragraph Map: Writing a Definition Paragraph

Topic sentence _____

_____

Point #1 _____

Narration _____

Point #2 _____

Example _____

Example _____

Point #3 _____

Example _____

Example _____

Concluding statement _____

_____

The following paragraph uses several patterns of development—including classification and exemplification—to define the term *happiness*.

Happiness

Although people disagree about what brings happiness, a feeling of contentment or joy, I know exactly what happiness means to me. The first kind of happiness is the result of money. It comes from unexpectedly finding a twenty-dollar bill in my pocket. It comes from hitting the jackpot on a slot machine after putting in just one quarter. The second kind of happiness comes from success. It comes from getting an A on a test or being told that my financial aid has been renewed for another year. Of course, I know that happiness is not just about money or success. The most valuable kind of happiness comes from the small things in life that make me feel good. This

Topic sentence includes formal definition

Transitions introduce three kinds of happiness

kind of happiness is taking the time to have a cup of coffee before class or eating lunch at an old-fashioned diner in my neighborhood. It is watching kids play Little League ball in the summer or playing pick-up basketball with my friends. It is finding out that I can still run a couple of miles even though I haven't exercised in a while or that I can still remember all the state capitals that I had to memorize in elementary school. For me, happiness is more than just money or success; it is the little things that bring joy to my life.

■ Concluding statement

— Edward Fernandez (student)

Transitions are important in definition paragraphs. The following box lists some transitional words and phrases that are used in definition paragraphs. In addition to these transitions, you can also use the transitional words and phrases for the pattern (or patterns) that you use to develop your definition paragraph.

Some Transitional Words and Phrases for Definition

also	one characteristic . . . another
first (second, third)	characteristic
for example	one way . . . another way
in addition	specifically
in particular	the first kind . . . the second kind
like	unlike

GRAMMAR IN CONTEXT

Definition

A definition paragraph often includes a formal definition of the term or idea you are going to discuss. When you write a formal definition, be careful not to use the phrase *is where* or *is when*.

Happiness is ~~when you have~~ a feeling of contentment or joy.

B Writing a Definition Paragraph

■ PRACTICE 12-1

Read this definition paragraph, and answer the questions that follow.

What Is a Bollywood Film?

Bollywood movies are popular films that are made in Mumbai, India. The term *Bollywood* is a combination of the words *Hollywood*, home of the U.S. movie industry, and *Bombay*, the former name for the city of Mumbai. Bollywood movies have several characteristics that Indian audiences want. First, most Bollywood movies are musicals. Song-and-dance scenes are essential. In most cases, the songs are prerecorded by professional singers, and the actors in the movie lip-synch the lyrics. The dancing may be in classical Indian style, or it may mix classical style with modern Western pop numbers. Second, the plot of a Bollywood movie is likely to be very complicated, with many surprises and coincidences. Many plots involve star-crossed lovers, angry parents, and love triangles. Third, Indian audiences want to get their money's worth. As a result, Bollywood movies are often over three hours long and offer a mixture of comedy and thrills in addition to the main plot. Because of their popularity, Bollywood movies have made the Indian movie industry the largest in the world.

— Megha Patel (student)

1. Underline the paragraph's topic sentence.

2. Does the topic sentence include a formal definition of the paragraph's subject? _____

3. List the three characteristics that the writer presents to help readers understand the nature of Bollywood movies.

    _____

    _____

    _____

4. What patterns of development does the writer use in the definition?

    _____

    _____

    _____

5. Underline the paragraph's concluding statement.

STRATEGIES FOR COLLEGE SUCCESS

Listening for Important Terms during a Lecture

During lectures, listen for important terms, which your instructor may emphasize by repeating them, by defining them, or by writing them on the board. Be sure to underline or circle these terms in your notes. For additional tips on how to become a successful student, see Chapter 1.

■ PRACTICE 12-2

Following are four topic sentences for definition paragraphs. Each sentence contains an underlined word or phrase. List two ways you could develop an extended definition of the underlined word or phrase.

1. <u>Surveillance cameras</u> help communities to fight crime.

   _____

   _____

2. <u>Terrorism</u> is a world-wide problem.

   _____

   _____

3. <u>Alternate energy sources</u> can help the United States become energy independent.

   _____

   _____

4. <u>A sense of humor</u> is an important quality for a person to have.

   _____

   _____

■ PRACTICE 12-3

Choose one of the topics below (or a topic of your own) as the subject of a definition paragraph.

A symbol of your religion
  (for example, a star,
  a crucifix, or a crescent)
A style of popular music
A technical term
A tool found in most
  households
A fad
Street sense

A term in a language other than
  English
A good day
Sexual harassment
Stress
An ideal mate
Freedom
A key concept or term
  in a course you are taking

■ PRACTICE 12-4

Use one of the strategies described in 3C to help you find information about the term you have chosen to define. Your goal is to list the item's features or characteristics. (You may also make notes about the item's origin or history or explain how it is like or unlike other similar things.)

■ PRACTICE 12-5

Review your notes from Practice 12-4. On the following lines, list the details that can help you develop a definition paragraph.

- _____
- _____
- _____
- _____
- _____
- _____

■ PRACTICE 12-6

On the lines below, list the ideas you will discuss in your paragraph, arranging them in an effective order.

1. _____
2. _____
3. _____
4. _____
5. _____

■ PRACTICE 12-7

Reread your list from Practice 12-5. Then, draft a topic sentence that states your main idea and includes a formal definition.

Topic sentence: _____

_____

_____

■ PRACTICE 12-8

Draft your definition paragraph.

■ PRACTICE 12-9

Using the Self-Assessment Checklist on page 182, revise your definition paragraph.

■ PRACTICE 12-10

Print out a final draft of your definition paragraph.

✓ Seeing and Writing: Skills Check

Look back at your response to the Seeing and Writing activity on page 175. Reread it, and answer the following questions:

- Is your paragraph unified?
- Is your paragraph well developed?
- Is your paragraph coherent?

Then, revise and edit your paragraph.

✓ Self-Assessment Checklist

Writing a Definition Paragraph

- ☐ Does your topic sentence state your paragraph's main idea?
- ☐ Does your topic sentence identify the term to be defined?
- ☐ Does your topic sentence include a formal definition?
- ☐ Have you developed the rest of the paragraph with one or more of the patterns of development discussed in this text?
- ☐ Have you used appropriate transitional words and phrases to introduce your points?
- ☐ Have you avoided using *is when* and *is where* in your definition?
- ☐ Have you included a concluding statement that sums up your paragraph's main idea?

CHAPTER REVIEW

1. The following student definition paragraph is missing a topic sentence, transitional words and phrases, and a concluding statement. After reading the paragraph (and possibly consulting a dictionary), fill in the missing elements on the appropriate lines below. (See p. 178 for a list of transitions.)

What Are Blogs?

_____

_____

Blogs first appeared in the 1990s and have exploded in popularity since then.

Blogs may be like online journals, including the blogger's thoughts about his

or her life. _____, they may comment on what is happening on the

Web or in the world. Some of the most popular blogs are *PerezHilton*, *Engadget*,

and *BoingBoing*. Usually, blog entries are listed in reverse chronological order,

with the most recent appearing first. _____ entries on a blog can be

unrelated. At other times, they can focus on a particular topic. _____

online journals, however, blogs often contain links to other sites. Although some

blog are very long, others may be just a sentence or two. _____, one

blogging tool, Twitter, limits entries—known as "tweets"—to 140 characters.

Posting videos alongside text is another trend in blogging. Because anyone

with an Internet connection can publish a blog, they vary in content and

quality. Some blogs have just a few readers. _____, those written

by popular media personalities may be read by thousands of people each day.

_____

_____

2. Create a definition paragraph by adding sentences to support the
   topic sentence below. Use several different patterns of development,
   and be sure to include transitional words and phrases to lead readers
   through your discussion and end the paragraph with a clear concluding statement. Finally, add an appropriate title on the line provided.

   _____

   Success is a concept that is difficult to define. _____

   _____

   _____

   _____

   _____

   _____

   _____

   _____

   _____

   _____

3. The pictures below show Americans from several different back-grounds. Look carefully at the pictures, and then write a paragraph in which you define the term *American*. How do the people in the pictures fit (or not fit) your definition? Begin your paragraph with a topic sentence that includes a formal definition of *American*. Then, in the rest of the paragraph, define the term by using any of the patterns of development discussed in this text.

Friends

A mixed-race family

An Indian American family

Latina girls showing off their dresses

Argument

CHAPTER 13

PREVIEW

In this chapter, you will learn to write an argument paragraph.

SEEING AND WRITING ▲

The picture above shows a scene from the classic 1969 film *Easy Rider.* Almost all U.S. states once had laws requiring motorcycle riders and passengers to wear helmets. Today, largely because of motorcyclists' objections, fewer than half of states have a helmet requirement. Look at the picture, and then write a paragraph in which you argue against a law that you consider unfair or unjust. Make sure you include the specific reasons that you object to the law you are discussing. Try to use the Word Power words in your paragraph.

185

A What Is Argument?

When most people hear the word *argument*, they think of the heated exchanges they hear on television interview programs or on radio talk shows. These discussions, however, are more like shouting matches than arguments.

A true **argument**—the kind you are expected to make in college—involves taking a well-thought-out position on a *debatable issue*—an issue on which reasonable people may disagree:

- Should intelligent design be taught in high school classrooms?
- Should teenagers who commit felonies be tried as adults?

In an argument, you attempt to convince people of the strength of your ideas not by shouting but by presenting **evidence**—facts and examples. In the process, you also consider opposing ideas, and if they are strong, you acknowledge their strengths. If your evidence is solid and your logic is sound, you will present a convincing argument.

ASSIGNMENTS FOR ARGUMENT

You will use argument in many of your college classes. Here are some typical assignments:

- *In a public health class:* Should medical marijuana be legalized?
- *In an ethics class:* Should every American be required by law to buy health insurance?
- *In a religion class:* In a multifaith society, should religious believers try to convert followers of other religions?
- *In a composition course:* Is it time to legalize gay marriage?
- *In a sports management course:* Are high salaries for players ruining Major League Baseball?
- *In a literature class:* Does the narrator in Tillie Olen's short story "I Stand Here Ironing" fail to live up to her role as a mother?

When you write an **argument paragraph**, your purpose is to persuade readers that your position has merit. To write an effective argument paragraph, follow these guidelines:

- *Write a topic sentence that clearly states your position.* Use words like *should, should not,* or *ought to* in your topic sentence to make your position clear to readers.

The federal government should lower the tax on gasoline.

The city should not build a new sports stadium.

- *Include points that support your topic sentence.* For example, if your purpose is to argue for placing warning labels on unhealthy snack foods, give several reasons why this would be a good idea.
- *Present convincing support.* Support each of your points with evidence (facts and examples).

FOCUS

Evidence

There are two kinds of evidence—*facts* and *examples*:

1. A **fact** is a piece of information that can be verified. If you make a point, you should be prepared to support it with facts—for example, statistics, observations, or statements that are accepted as true.

2. An **example** is a specific illustration of a general statement. To be convincing, an example should be clearly related to the point you are making.

- *Identify and address opposing arguments.* Try to imagine what your opponent's arguments might be, and explain how they are inaccurate or weak. By addressing these objections in your paragraph, you strengthen your position.
- *Write a strong concluding statement.* A concluding statement reinforces the main idea of your paragraph. In an argument paragraph, it is especially important to summarize the position you introduced in your topic sentence.

Paragraph Map: Writing an Argument Paragraph

Topic sentence _____

_____

Point #1 _____

_____

Point #2 _____

_____

Point #3 _____

_____

Opposing argument #1 _____

_____

Opposing argument #2 _____

_____

Concluding statement _____

_____

The following argument paragraph presents three reasons to support the writer's position.

Taxing Soda

Topic sentence

Recently, some people have suggested taxing soda because they think it is not healthy for young people. I am against this tax because it is unfair, it is unnecessary, and it won't work. The first reason this kind of tax is bad is that it is not fair. The American Medical Association (AMA) thinks the tax will fight obesity in the United States. However, people should be allowed to decide for themselves whether they should drink soda. It is not right for a group of doctors to decide what is best for everybody.

Transitions introduce points that support the topic sentence

Another reason this kind of tax is bad is that it is unnecessary. It would be better to set up educational programs to help children make decisions about what they eat. In addition, the AMA could educate parents so they will stop buying soda for their children. Education will do more to help children than a tax will. Finally, this kind of tax is bad because it won't work. As long as soda is for sale, children will drink it. The only thing that will work is outlawing soda completely, and no one is suggesting this.

Transitions introduce opposing arguments

Of course, some people say that soda should be taxed because it has no nutritional value. This is true, but many snack foods have little nutritional value, and no one is proposing a tax on snack food. In addition, not everyone who drinks soda is overweight, let alone obese. A tax on soda would hurt everyone, including people who are healthy and don't drink it

Concluding statement

very often. The key to helping young people is not to tax them but to teach them what a healthy diet is.

— Ashley Hale (student)

Transitions are important for argument paragraphs. The following box lists the transitional words and phrases that are commonly used in argument paragraphs. Some transitions—*first, second,* and so on—indicate that you are moving from one point to another. Others—*of course, in addition,* and so on—introduce opposing arguments.

Some Transitional Words and Phrases for Argument

accordingly	finally	on the one hand . . .
admittedly	however	on the other hand
although	in addition	since
because	in conclusion	the first reason . . .
but	in fact	another reason
certainly	in summary	therefore
consequently	meanwhile	thus
despite	moreover	to be sure
even so	nevertheless	truly
even though	nonetheless	
first . . . second . . .	of course	

GRAMMAR IN CONTEXT

Argument

When you write an argument paragraph, you need to show the relationships among your ideas. You do this by combining simple sentences to create compound and complex sentences.

COMPOUND SENTENCE The only thing that will work is outlawing soda *, and no* completely. ~~No~~ one is suggesting this.

COMPLEX SENTENCE Recently, some people have suggested taxing *because they* soda. ~~They~~ think it is not healthy for young people.

For more information on how to create compound sentences, see Chapter 16. For more information on how to create complex sentences, see Chapter 17.

B Writing an Argument Paragraph

PRACTICE 13-1

Read this argument paragraph, and answer the questions that follow it.

The Importance of Voting

Many American citizens never cast a ballot, and voter turnout is often below 50 percent even in presidential elections. It is sad that people give up this hard-won right. It is in every citizen's best interest to vote. One reason to vote is that government affects every part of our lives. It is foolish not to have a say about who makes the laws and regulations people have to live with.

If a citizen does not vote, he or she has no voice on issues such as taxes, schools, health care, the environment, and even the building and repairing of roads and bridges. Another reason to vote is to support a particular political party. If a person believes in a party's policies, it is important to vote to elect that party's candidates and keep them in power. A third reason to vote is that voting enables people to influence public policy. Many people seem to think a single vote doesn't matter, but even if a voter's candidate does not win, his or her vote isn't wasted. The voter has expressed an opinion by voting, and the government in power is affected by public opinion. To keep our democracy working, all citizens should exercise their right to vote.

— Lori Wessier (student)

1. Underline the paragraph's topic sentence. Why do you think the writer places the topic sentence where she does?

_____

_____

_____

_____

2. What issue is the writer addressing?

_____

_____

_____

_____

What is the writer's position on the issue?

_____

_____

3. List some of the reasons the writer uses to support her position. The first reason has been listed for you.

The most important reason to vote is that government affects every part

of our lives. _____

_____

_____

_____

4. Where does the writer address an opposing argument?

_____

_____

_____

_____

5. Underline the paragraph's concluding statement.

STRATEGIES FOR COLLEGE SUCCESS

Evaluating Web Sites

Before using information you find online, consider some questions. Is the information you find on a site supported by facts and expert opinion? Is it up-to-date? Is it written by an authority on the subject? Does the author have a hidden purpose, such as selling a product? For additional tips on how to become a successful student, see Chapter 1.

■ PRACTICE 13-2

Following are four topic sentences for argument paragraphs. For each statement, list three points that could support the statement. For example, if you were arguing in favor of banning smoking in all public places, you could say that smoking is a nuisance, a health risk, and a fire hazard.

1. The dangers of global warming have been overstated.

_____

_____

_____

2. Becoming a volunteer in your community can be personally and professionally rewarding.

_____

_____

_____

3. High school students should be required to take four years of a foreign language.

_____

_____

_____

4. Congress should act at once to increase the minimum wage.

_____

_____

_____

PRACTICE 13-3

Choose one of the following topics (or a topic of your own) as the subject of an argument paragraph.

Why you would be a good president

Should illegal immigrants be given amnesty?

Is a college education necessary for success?

Is our right to privacy being lost?

Why a particular improvement is needed in your town

A policy or requirement that should be changed at your school

Should prayer be allowed in public schools?

Is space exploration a waste of time and money?

Should radio talk shows be required to present both sides of an issue?

An environmental issue

A health-care issue

Safety on your campus

Financial aid policies at your school

Should same-sex couples have the right to marry?

Should assisted suicide be legal?

Should cigarettes be illegal?

PRACTICE 13-4

Once you have chosen an issue in Practice 13-3, write a journal entry exploring your position on the issue. Consider the following questions:

- What is your position?
- Why do you feel the way you do?
- What specific actions do you think should be taken?
- What objections might be raised against your position?
- How might you respond to these objections?

PRACTICE 13-5

Review your journal entry, and make some additional notes about the issue you have chosen. Then, select the points that best support your position. List the points below. After you have finished, list the strongest objections to your position.

Supporting points:

- _____

- _____

- _____
- _____

Objections:

- _____

- _____

■ PRACTICE 13-6

Review the supporting points you listed in Practice 13-5. Then, draft a topic sentence that clearly expresses the position you will take in your paragraph.

Topic sentence: _____

_____

■ PRACTICE 13-7

On the lines below, list the points that support your position, arranging them in an effective order (for example, from least to most important).

1. _____
2. _____
3. _____
4. _____
5. _____

■ PRACTICE 13-8

Draft your argument paragraph.

■ PRACTICE 13-9

Using the Self-Assessment Checklist on page 194, revise your argument paragraph.

■ PRACTICE 13-10

Print out a final draft of your argument paragraph.

✓ Seeing and Writing: Skills Check

Look back at your response to the Seeing and Writing activity on page 185. Reread it, and answer the following questions:

- Is your paragraph unified?
- Is your paragraph well developed?
- Is your paragraph coherent?

Then, revise and edit your paragraph.

✓ Self-Assessment Checklist

Writing an Argument Paragraph

☐ Does your topic sentence clearly state your position?

☐ Do you support your points with specific facts and examples?

☐ Have you identified and addressed opposing arguments?

☐ Have you used appropriate transitional words and phrases to introduce your points and to identify opposing arguments?

☐ Have you used compound and complex sentences to show how your ideas are related?

☐ Have you included a concluding statement that reinforces the main idea of your paragraph?

CHAPTER REVIEW

1. The following student argument paragraph is missing a topic sentence, transitional words and phrases, and a concluding statement. After reading the paragraph, fill in the missing elements on the appropriate lines below. (See p. 189 for a list of transitions.)

Stop Animal Experimentation

_____. The work done by

scientists on animal behavior suggests that animals feel, think, and even

communicate with each other. _____, work with whales and dolphins

shows that these animals can be trained and can also think. For instance,

researchers have found that dolphins identify themselves with unique whistles.

These whistles allow each dolphin to be distinguished from others over great distances. _____, it seems that the gap between human beings and the rest of the animal kingdom is getting smaller. _____, wild chimpanzees have been seen using tools to pry termites out of termite mounds. _____, some chimps have been taught to use sign language. _____ many people assume that animals cannot grieve, some animals have been observed mourning their dead. _____, elephants may stand for hours around a dead member of their clan, touching the body with their trunks and feet. _____, some animals, such as mice, are not as intelligent as dolphins or elephants. _____, research has shown that they can react to positive and negative emotions in other mice. These developments are making it increasingly difficult to justify animal experiments. _____, some people will say that animal experimentation is necessary to save human lives. _____, experts point out that many, if not most, experiments currently done with animals can be duplicated with computer models. _____

_____.

2. Create an argument paragraph by adding several points to support the topic sentence below. Be sure to include transitional words and phrases to introduce your points. If possible, try to address at least one argument against your position, and end the paragraph with a clear concluding statement. Finally, add an appropriate title.

_____

Hitting children is never a good way to discipline them. _____

_____

_____

_____

_____

_____

_____

_____

3. A number of states have passed laws restricting the rights of undocumented immigrants. Look carefully at the picture, and write a paragraph in which you argue either that these restrictions are a good idea or that they violate rights that all people should have, regardless of their immigration status. Begin your paragraph with a topic sentence that states your position. Then, in the rest of the paragraph, present evidence to support your position.

Writing an Essay

PREVIEW

In this chapter, you will learn

- to understand essay structure (**14A**)
- to focus on your assignment, purpose, and audience (**14B**)
- to find ideas to write about (**14C**)
- to identify your main idea and state your thesis (**14D**)
- to choose and arrange your supporting points (**14E**)
- to draft your essay (**14F**)
- to revise and edit your essay (**14G**)

SEEING AND WRITING ▲

Look at the picture above, which shows a roller derby match. Then, write a paragraph in which you consider whether there is too much violence in some sports. Try to use the Word Power words in your paragraph.

WORD POWER

brawl: a noisy fight

conflict: a disagreement or clash

altercation: a quarrel

A   Understanding Essay Structure

In the previous chapters, we have been discussing paragraphs. Now, we will discuss essays. An **essay** is a group of paragraphs about one subject. In this chapter, you will see how the strategies you learned for writing paragraphs can also help you write essays.

In some ways, essays and paragraphs are similar. For example, both paragraphs and essays have a single **main idea**.

As you have learned, a paragraph's main idea is stated in a **topic sentence**, and the rest of the paragraph supports this main idea. The paragraph often ends with a concluding statement that sums up the main idea.

Paragraph

The **topic sentence** states the main idea of the paragraph.

Support develops the main idea with details and examples.

The **concluding statement** sums up the main idea.

In an essay, the main idea is presented in a **thesis statement**. The first paragraph—the **introduction**—includes the thesis statement. The main part of the essay consists of several **body paragraphs** that support the thesis statement. The essay ends with a **conclusion** that restates the thesis (in different words) and brings the essay to a close. This essay structure is called **thesis and support**.

Thesis-and-Support Essay

Introduction —

Opening remarks introduce the subject to be discussed.

The **thesis statement** presents the main idea of the essay in the last sentence of the first paragraph.

Body paragraphs —

Topic sentence (first point)

Support (details and examples)

Topic sentence (second point)

Support (details and examples)

— Body paragraphs

Topic sentence (third point)

Support (details and examples)

The **restatement of the thesis** summarizes the essay's main idea.

— Conclusion

Closing remarks present the writer's last thoughts on the subject.

Here is an essay that follows this thesis-and-support structure.

My Grandfather's Lessons

My grandfather, Richard Weaver, is seventy years old and lives in Leola, a small town outside of Lancaster, Pennsylvania. He has lived there his entire life. As a young man, he apprenticed as a stone mason and eventually started his own business. He worked as a stone mason until he got silicosis and had to retire. He now works part time for the local water department. When I was eight, my mother was very sick, and I lived with my grandparents for almost a year. During that time, my grandfather taught me some important lessons about life.

One thing my grandfather taught me was that I did not have to spend money or go places to have a good time. An afternoon in his workshop was more than enough to keep me entertained. We spent many hours together working on small projects, such as building a wagon, and large projects, such as building a tree house. My grandfather even designed a pulley system that carried me from the roof of his house to the tree house. Working next to my

Opening remarks

— Introduction

Thesis statement

Topic sentence

Support
— First body paragraph

grandfather, I also learned the value of patience and hard work. He never cut corners or compromised. He taught me that it was easier to do the job right the first time than to do it twice.

Topic sentence

Support

Second body paragraph

Another thing my grandfather taught me was the importance of helping others. Whenever anyone needs help, my grandfather is always there — whatever the cost or personal inconvenience. One afternoon a year ago, a friend called him from work and asked him to help fix a broken water pipe. My grandfather immediately canceled his plans and went to help. When he was a member of the volunteer fire department, my grandfather refused to quit even though my grandmother thought the job was too dangerous. His answer was typical of him: he said that people depended on him, and he could not let them down.

Topic sentence

Support

Third body paragraph

The most important thing my grandfather taught me was that honesty is its own reward. One day, when my grandfather and I were in a mall, I found a wallet. I held it up and proudly showed it to my grandfather. When I opened it up and saw the money inside, I couldn't believe it. I had wanted a mountain bike for the longest time, but every time I had asked my grandfather for one, he had told me to be thankful for what I already had. So when I saw the money, I thought that my prayers had been answered. My grandfather, however, had other ideas. He told me that we would have to call the owner of the wallet and tell him that we had found it. Later that night, we called the owner (his name was on his driver's license inside the wallet), and he came over to pick up his money. As soon as I saw him, I knew that my grandfather was right. The man looked as if he really needed the money. When he offered me a reward, I told him no. After he left, my grandfather told me how proud of me he was.

Restatement of thesis

Conclusion

Closing remarks

The lessons I learned from my grandfather — doing a job right, helping others, and being honest — were important. Now that I have grown up, I have adopted these special qualities of his. I hope that someday I can pass them on to my own children and grandchildren the way my grandfather passed them on to me.

14 B

201
Focusing on Your
Assignment,
Purpose, and
Audience

The rest of this chapter explains the process of writing a thesis-and-support essay. Keep in mind that although the steps in the process are discussed one at a time, they often overlap. For example, while you are writing your first draft, you may also be trying to find more ideas to write about.

B Focusing on Your Assignment, Purpose, and Audience

Most of the essays you write in college will be in response to assignments that your instructors give you. Before you can begin to write about these assignments, however, you need to determine why you are expected to write (your **purpose**) and for whom you will be writing (your **audience**). Once you understand your purpose and audience, you are ready to focus on your **assignment**.

In your writing class, you may be given general assignments such as the following ones:

- Discuss something your school could do to improve the lives of returning older students.
- Examine a decision you made that changed your life.
- Write about the problems (or advantages) of social-networking sites.

Before you can respond to these general assignments, you will need to ask yourself some questions. Exactly what could your school do to improve the lives of older students? What decision did you make that changed your life? Exactly what dangers or benefits of social-networking sites do you want to discuss? By asking yourself questions like these, you can narrow these general assignments to specific **topics** that you can write about:

- Free day care on campus
- My struggle to give up smoking
- The dangers of Facebook

■ PRACTICE 14-1 ■

The following topics are too general for a short essay. On the line that follows each assignment topic, narrow the topic down so it is suitable for a brief essay.

Example: A personal problem

How I learned to deal with stress

_____

1. A problem at your school

_____

2. Blended families

_____

3. Unwanted presents

_____

4. Current styles of body art

_____

5. Censorship

_____

C Finding Ideas to Write About

Once you have a topic, you need to find ideas to write about. You do this by using _freewriting_, _brainstorming_, _clustering_, or _journal writing_—just as you do when you write a paragraph.

▨ PRACTICE 14-2 ▨

Reread the Seeing and Writing activity on page 197, and review section 3C of this text. Then, use whatever strategies you like—such as _freewriting_ or _brainstorming_—to help you think of material for your essay on violence in sports. If your instructor gives you permission, you may discuss your ideas with other students.

D Identifying Your Main Idea and Stating Your Thesis

After you have decided on a topic and gathered material to write about, you need to look through your material to find a main idea that it can support. You are then ready to write a **thesis statement**—a single sentence that clearly states the main idea that you will discuss in the rest of your essay.

Topic	_Thesis Statement_
Free day care on campus	Free day care on campus would improve the lives of the many students who are also parents.
My struggle to give up smoking	Giving up smoking was hard, but it saved me money and gave me self-respect.
The dangers of Facebook	Despite its popularity, Facebook creates some serious problems.

14 D

203
Identifying Your
Main Idea and
Stating Your
Thesis

Like a topic sentence, a thesis statement tells readers what to expect. An effective thesis statement does two things:

- *An effective thesis statement makes a point about your topic.* For this reason, it must do more than simply state a fact or announce what you plan to write about.

  STATEMENT OF FACT   Free day care is not available on our campus.

  ANNOUNCEMENT   In this essay, I will discuss free day care on campus.

  EFFECTIVE THESIS STATEMENT   Free day care on campus would improve the lives of the many students who are also parents.

- *An effective thesis statement is specific and clearly worded.*

  VAGUE THESIS STATEMENT   Giving up smoking helped me a lot.

  EFFECTIVE THESIS STATEMENT   Giving up smoking was hard, but it saved me money and gave me self-respect.

FOCUS

Stating Your Thesis

At this stage of the writing process, your thesis is **tentative**, not definite. As you write and revise, you are likely to change it—possibly several times.

▮ PRACTICE 14-3 ▮

In the space provided, indicate whether each of the following items is a fact (*F*), an announcement (*A*), a vague statement (*VS*), or an effective thesis (*ET*). If your instructor gives you permission, you can break into groups and do this exercise collaboratively.

Examples

Domestic violence is a problem. __*VS*__

The federal government should provide more funding for programs that help victims of domestic violence. __*ET*__

1. Americans have a life expectancy of more than seventy-seven years.

   _____

2. There are several reasons why life expectancy has risen in the past century. _____

3. Slavery was a bad practice. _____

4. In 2009, the minimum wage was raised to $7.25 an hour. _____

5. An increase in the federal minimum wage is necessary. _____

6. In this essay, I will describe some funny incidents that occurred when my father went camping. _____

7. Most Americans say they believe in God. _____

8. Religious institutions can help drug addicts in three ways. _____

9. The post office is really slow. _____

10. Email has some clear advantages over regular mail. _____

▨ PRACTICE 14-4 ▨

Carefully review the material you have gathered for your essay about violence in sports. Then, write a tentative thesis statement for your essay on the lines below.

Tentative thesis statement: _____

_____

E Choosing and Arranging Your Supporting Points

After you have decided on a tentative thesis statement, your next step is to identify the points you will discuss and list them in the order in which you intend to write about them. For example, you might arrange the points from most general to most specific or from least important to most important. You can use this list of points as a rough outline for your essay.

▨ PRACTICE 14-5 ▨

Review the tentative thesis statement you wrote in Practice 14-4. Then, review the material you came up with in Practice 14-2, and decide which points you will use to support your thesis statement. List those points on the lines below.

_____

_____

_____

_____

_____

_____

Now, arrange these points in the order in which you plan to write about them. Cross out any points that do not support your thesis statement.

1. _____

2. _____

3. _____

4. _____

5. _____

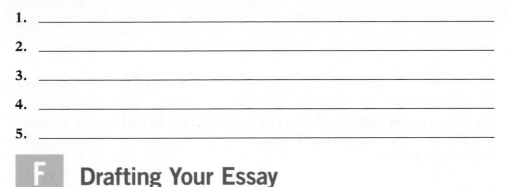 # F Drafting Your Essay

After you have decided on a thesis and have arranged your points in the order in which you will present them, you are ready to draft your essay.

Keep in mind that you are writing a rough draft, one that you will revise and edit later. Your goal at this point is simply to get your ideas down so that you can react to them. Even so, your draft should have a thesis-and-support structure.

Here is the first draft of an essay by Anna Habos, a student in an introductory writing class. Before she wrote her essay, Anna went through the process discussed in this chapter.

The Trouble with Facebook

Using Facebook is a good way to keep up with friends. Facebook makes it easy to invite people to parties, share photographs, connect with others, and announce big news. However, despite its popularity, Facebook creates some serious problems.

Facebook can interrupt school or work. Email alerts from Facebook can become a major distraction. Once on the site, a person can get sucked into all the activities that are available. It is easy to waste time on Facebook.

Posting inappropriate comments or pictures can have serious consequences. For example, it can lead to being fired, denied admission to a school, or not offered a job. In addition, friends may embarrass each other on Facebook. In most cases, they do not mean to, but they accidentally say something wrong.

One major mistake people make on Facebook is revealing too much information. Listing addresses, phone numbers, hobbies, or a current work address can lead to problems. A stranger with bad intentions can use this information to track down someone to stalk or rob.

Despite these drawbacks, it is possible to use Facebook responsibly and safely. Because I understand the trouble with Facebook, I feel confident using the site.

■ PRACTICE 14-6

Reread Anna Habos's first draft. What changes would you suggest she make? What might she add? What might she delete? Write your suggestions on the following lines. (If your instructor gives you permission, you can break into groups and do this exercise collaboratively.)

_____

_____

_____

_____

_____

PRACTICE 14-7

Write a draft of your essay about violence in sports. Be sure to include the thesis statement you drafted in Practice 14-4 as well as the points you listed in the last part of Practice 14-5. When you are finished, give your essay a title.

G Revising and Editing Your Essay

When you **revise** your essay, you reconsider the choices you made when you wrote your first draft. As a result, you rethink (and frequently rewrite) parts of your essay. Some of your changes will be major—for example, deleting several sentences or even crossing out or adding whole paragraphs. Other changes will be minor—for example, adding or deleting a word or phrase.

Before you begin to revise, try to put your essay aside for at least an hour or two. Time away from your essay will help you distance yourself from your writing so you can see it critically. When you start to revise, don't be afraid to mark up your first draft with lines, arrows, and cross-outs or to write between the lines and in the margins.

When you are finished revising, **edit** your essay, concentrating on grammar, punctuation, mechanics, and spelling.

✓ Self-Assessment Checklist

Editing Your Essay

Editing for Common Sentence Problems:

☐ Have you avoided run-ons? (See Chapter 20.)

☐ Have you avoided sentence fragments? (See Chapter 21.)

☐ Do your subjects and verbs agree? (See Chapter 22.)

☐ Have you avoided illogical shifts? (See Chapter 23.)

☐ Have you avoided dangling and misplaced modifiers? (See Chapter 24.)

Editing for Grammar:

☐ Are your verb forms and verb tenses correct? (See Chapters 25 and 26.)

☐ Have you used nouns and pronouns correctly? (See Chapters 27 and 28.)

☐ Have you used adjectives and adverbs correctly? (See Chapter 29.)

Editing for Punctuation, Mechanics, and Spelling:

☐ Have you used commas correctly? (See Chapter 31.)

☐ Have you used apostrophes correctly? (See Chapter 32.)

☐ Have you used other punctuation correctly? (See Chapter 33.)

☐ Have you used capital letters where they are required? (See Chapter 34.)

☐ Have you used quotation marks correctly where they are needed? (See Chapter 34.)

☐ Have you spelled every word correctly? (See Chapter 35.)

FOCUS

Choosing a Title

Every essay should have a **title** that suggests the subject of the essay and makes people want to read it.

As you choose a title for your paper, think about the following options:

- *A title can highlight a key word or term.*
  Tortillas
  Learning Tagalog

- *A title can be a straightforward announcement.*
  Photographs of My Parents
  Before Air Conditioning

- *A title can establish a personal connection with readers.*
  Do What You Love
  America, Stand Up for Justice and Democracy

- *A title can be a familiar saying or a quotation from your essay itself.*
  The Dog Ate My Disk, and Other Tales of Woe

When you write your title, keep the following guidelines in mind:

- Capitalize all words except for articles (*a, an, the*), prepositions (*at, to, of, around,* and so on), and coordinating conjunctions (*and, but,* and so on), unless they are the first or last word of the title.

- Do not underline or italicize your title or enclose it in quotation marks.

- Center the title at the top of the first page. Double-space between the title and the first line of your essay.

STRATEGIES FOR COLLEGE SUCCESS

Writing Essay Exams

On a timed essay exam, your instructor will often expect you to write a thesis-and-support essay. Remember to structure your essay around a clearly stated main idea. You should present this main idea in a thesis statement, support it in several body paragraphs, and conclude by restating it. For additional tips on how to become a successful student, see Chapter 1.

✓ **Self-Assessment Checklist**

Revising Your Essay

☐ Does your essay have an introduction, a body, and a conclusion?

☐ Does your introduction include a clearly worded thesis statement?

☐ Does your thesis statement present your essay's main idea?

☐ Does each body paragraph have a topic sentence?

☐ Does each body paragraph focus on one point that supports the thesis statement?

☐ Does each body paragraph include details and examples that support the topic sentence?

☐ Does your conclusion include a restatement of your thesis?

When Anna Habos revised her essay about Facebook, she decided to change her thesis statement so that it was more specific and better reflected what she wanted to say. In addition, she added topic sentences to focus her paragraphs and to help readers see how her body paragraphs related to her thesis statement. To make these relationships clear, she added transitional words and phrases (*one way; another way; the most important way*). She also added examples to make her discussion more interesting and more convincing. (She took some examples from her journal and some from her personal knowledge of Facebook.) Finally, she expanded her introduction and conclusion.

After she finished revising and editing her essay, Anna proofread it to correct any errors in spelling, grammar, and punctuation that she might have missed. Finally, she checked to make sure that her essay followed her instructor's guidelines.

FOCUS

Guidelines for Submitting Your Papers

Always follow your instructor's guidelines for submitting papers.

- Unless your instructor tells you otherwise, type your name, your instructor's name, the course name and number, and the date (day, month, year) in the upper left-hand corner of your paper's first page, one-half inch from the top.
- Print on one side of each sheet of paper.
- Double-space your work.
- Leave one-inch margins on all sides of the page.
- Type your last name and the page number in the upper right-hand corner of each page (including the first page).

Here is the final draft of Anna's essay.

Anna Habos
Professor Smith
Composition 101
18 November 2010

Habos 1

The Trouble with Facebook

Facebook is a popular way for busy people — particularly students — to keep up with friends. This social-networking site makes it easy for them to invite people to parties, share photographs, connect with others, and announce big news. However, because communicating on the site is so easy, some students get themselves into difficulty. To avoid problems, students should be aware of the dangers they can face when they use Facebook.

One way students can get into trouble is by letting Facebook distract them from school or work. If they are not careful, they can let email alerts draw them into Facebook over and over again throughout the day. For example, alerts may tell users whenever a new comment is posted on one of their conversations. If users respond to all these alerts, they will find themselves spending an excessive amount of time online socializing with their "friends" instead of studying or working. Even Facebook users who do not use email alerts still log in frequently just to stay up-to-date. Once on the site, students can waste a lot of valuable

Opening remarks

Thesis statement

Topic sentence

Support

time. For example, during a recent visit to Facebook, I spent forty minutes reviewing new posts, updating my status, and responding to a friend's message.

Topic sentence

Support

Another way students can get into trouble on Facebook is by sharing personal thoughts and photographs too freely. An off-color comment or a revealing photograph posted on the site may seem harmless. However, a boss, a human resources employee, or a college admissions officer may not see these posts as meaningless fun. To them, they may indicate that a person is immature, unreliable, or unmotivated—in short, someone who cannot be trusted to act responsibly. Thus, inappropriate posts can damage a student professionally as well as personally. Of course, it is fine to reveal a personal secret on the phone to a friend. However, posting the same secret on a Facebook page that can be accessed by hundreds of friends, acquaintances, coworkers, and potential employers might be both hurtful and embarrassing.

Topic sentence

Support

The most serious way students can get into trouble on Facebook is by revealing too much about themselves—for example, by posting addresses, phone numbers, employment information, and interests and hobbies. Posting this kind of information is particularly dangerous for women. For example, if a woman indicates that she lives in a particular small town and likes bowling, a stalker might go to the local bowling alley to look for her. Even worse, if a woman accepts a Facebook invitation to a party, a stranger will know exactly where and when to find her. Finally, sexual predators frequently search Facebook pages. As a result, many young adults—and even children—have been tricked into starting online relationships with adults who pose as teenagers. In some cases, these adults were sex offenders who used Facebook to locate victims. By revealing personal information, young Facebook users made it possible for these predators to find and harm them.

Restatement of thesis

Closing remarks

Despite these drawbacks, it is possible to use Facebook both responsibly and safely. Students should not allow Facebook activities to intrude excessively into their school day or workplace. They should think twice before posting comments that could hurt themselves or others. Finally, they should be careful about revealing personal information. By taking a few simple

Habos 3

precautions, students who use Facebook can enjoy social networking and still

be reasonably certain that people who access their pages will not be able to

harm them personally or professionally.

■ PRACTICE 14-8 ■

What did Anna add to her draft? What did she delete? What other
changes could she have made? Write your suggestions on the following lines.

_____

_____

_____

_____

_____

_____

✓ Seeing and Writing: Skills Check

Look back at your response to the Seeing and Writing activity on
page 197. Reread it, and complete the following tasks:

■ Using the Self-Assessment Checklist for revising your essay on
page 208 as a guide, evaluate the essay on violence in sports
that you wrote in response to the Seeing and Writing prompt.

■ On the following lines, list any changes you think you
should make to your draft.

_____

_____

_____

_____

■ Revise the draft of your essay.
■ Edit the revised draft, using the Self-Assessment Checklist
for editing your essay on page 206. Look for errors in grammar, punctuation, mechanics, and spelling.

CHAPTER REVIEW

EDITING PRACTICE

After reading the following incomplete student essay, write a thesis statement on the lines provided. (Make sure the thesis statement clearly communicates the essay's main idea.) Next, fill in the topic sentences for the second, third, and fourth paragraphs. Finally, restate the thesis (in different words) in the conclusion.

To Praise or Not to Praise

When I was growing up, praise was something children had to earn. It was not handed out lightly. Because I felt that more praise would have meant greater self-esteem, I promised myself I would praise my own children every chance I got. However, ten years of experience as a parent has changed my views. I have now come to realize that too much praise, given too easily, is not good. [Thesis statement]

_____

_____

_____

[Topic sentence] _____

_____

_____

_____

A father teaching his son to ride a bike.

When children feel they are valued, they learn more easily and work harder when the going gets tough. Self-doubt makes children too frightened of failure to take risks and overcome obstacles. When my older son, Tim, was a preschooler, I gave him lots of praise to build his self-esteem. My strategy worked. He is now a confident fifth-grader who does well in school and has many friends. I did the same for Zachary, who is six, with the same good results.

[Topic sentence] _____

_____

_____

_____

Parent scolding child

When you praise children, they know what is expected of them. They develop a set of inner rules, called a conscience, that with luck will last a lifetime. I believe that praise works better than criticism in molding a child's behavior. For example, when Tim was jealous of his newborn baby brother, my husband and I did not respond with criticism or threats. Instead, we encouraged Tim to help take care of the baby and praised him for doing so. He caught on, and his jealousy disappeared. If we had criticized or threatened him, I am sure his natural jealousy of the baby would have gotten worse.

[Topic sentence] _____

_____

_____

One of the harmful effects of praising my children too much was that they did not continue working on anything once they were praised for it. If I told them a first draft of a report or a drawing or a kite they were making was good, they put it aside and stopped working on it. Then they would get angry if I tried to get them to improve their work. I finally learned not to praise things that needed more effort. I learned to say things like, "Tell me more about the topic of this report. It's interesting. What else do you know about it?" It took a while before I learned how to say things so that I was not criticizing the children but also was not overpraising them.

[Restatement of thesis] _____

_____

_____

_____

My children seem to be less dependent on praise than they used to be, and they work harder at getting things right. I hope to use these new techniques in my future career as a preschool teacher and also teach them to other parents.

COLLABORATIVE ACTIVITIES

1. Working with another student, find an article in a magazine or a newspaper about a controversial issue that interests both of you. Then, identify the thesis statement of the article and the main points used to support that thesis. Underline topic sentences that state these points, and make a list of the details and examples that support each topic sentence. How does the article use the thesis-and-support structure to discuss the issue? How could the article be improved?

2. Working in a small group, develop thesis statements suitable for essays on two of the following topics.

   True friendship
   Professional athletes' salaries
   Censoring the Internet
   The value of volunteer work
   A course I will always remember
   Improving the public schools
   An essential electronic gadget
   A community problem

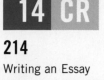

3. Choose one of the thesis statements you wrote for activity 2. Working with another student, make a list of at least three points that could be used to support the thesis.

✓ **Review Checklist**

Writing an Essay

☐ Many essays have a thesis-and-support structure: the thesis statement presents the main idea, and the body paragraphs support the thesis. (See 14A.)

☐ Begin by focusing on your assignment, purpose, and audience. (See 14B.)

☐ Narrow your general assignment to a topic you can write about. (See 14B.)

☐ Use one or more strategies to find ideas to write about. (See 14C.)

☐ State your main idea in a thesis statement. (See 14D.)

☐ List the points that best support your thesis, and arrange them in the order in which you plan to discuss them. (See 14E.)

☐ As you write your first draft, make sure your essay has a thesis-and-support structure. (See 14F.)

☐ Revise and edit your essay. (See 14G.)

UNIT THREE

Writing Effective Sentences

Writing Simple Sentences

CHAPTER 15

PREVIEW

In this chapter, you will learn

- to identify a sentence's subject (**15A**)
- to recognize singular and plural subjects (**15B**)
- to identify prepositions and prepositional phrases (**15C**)
- to distinguish a prepositional phrase from a subject (**15C**)
- to identify action verbs (**15D**)
- to identify linking verbs (**15E**)
- to identify helping verbs (**15F**)

SEEING AND WRITING ▲

If you met a person who had never been to McDonald's, what would you tell him or her about this fast-food restaurant? The picture above shows a typical McDonald's restaurant. Look at the picture, and then write a paragraph that answers this question. Try to use the Word Power words in your paragraph.

WORD POWER

institution: a well-known person, place, or thing

nutrition: a process by which a body uses food for growth

217

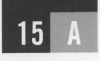

A **sentence** is a group of words that expresses a complete thought. Every sentence includes both a <u>subject</u> and a <u>verb</u>. A **simple sentence** consists of a single **independent clause**—one <u>subject</u> and one <u>verb</u>.

SUBJECT _r VERB

<u>McDonald's</u> <u><u>is</u></u> an American institution.

A Identifying Subjects

The **subject** of a sentence tells who or what is being talked about in the sentence.

Marissa did research on the Internet.
A reference librarian helped her find a topic for her paper.
It was due in March.

The subject of a sentence can be a noun or a pronoun. A **noun** names a person, place, or thing—*Marissa, librarian*. A **pronoun** takes the place of a noun—*I, you, he, she, it, we, they*.

PRACTICE 15-1

On the lines below, write in a subject (a noun or pronoun) that tells who or what is being talked about in the sentence.

> **Example:** The ____*wind*____ howled.

1. _____ was terrified.

2. The fierce _____ was very loud.

3. _____ banged on the roof.

4. A wild _____ barked in the distance.

5. Suddenly, a _____ rapped on the window.

6. _____ screamed and ran to the door.

7. Opening the door, _____ saw a frightening sight.

8. _____ closed the door immediately.

9. Outside, the howling _____ grew stronger.

10. Finally, _____ and _____ arrived.

FOCUS

Simple and Complete Subjects

A sentence's **simple subject** is just a noun or a pronoun.

Marissa   librarian   it

A sentence's **complete subject** is the simple subject along with all the words that describe it.

a reference librarian

NOTE: A two-word name, such as *Marissa Johnson*, is a simple subject.

■ PRACTICE 15-2

Underline each sentence's simple subject—the noun or pronoun that tells who or what the sentence is about. Then, put brackets around the complete subject.

Example: Today, [mobile <u>phones</u>] are an important part of our culture.

(1) Cell phones have changed a lot over the years. (2) Some people still remember the huge cell phone that Michael Douglas carried in the 1987 film *Wall Street*. (3) Few Americans had cell phones then. (4) Now, even some children have their own phones. (5) The first cell phones were bulky and had large antennae. (6) They were for talking only. (7) By the late 1990s, however, several manufacturers had introduced improvements. (8) The bulky handsets were gone. (9) Some phones offered music storage, Web access, and GPS features. (10) Since 2000, major advancements have included color displays, touch screens, cameras, video recorders, and apps.

■ PRACTICE 15-3

The following sentences have no subjects. Fill in each line below with a complete subject—a simple subject along with all the words that describe it. Remember to begin each sentence with a capital letter.

Example: ___My energetic sister___ runs a small business.

1. _____ crashed through the picture window.

2. _____ is my least favorite food.

3. _____ gave the players a pep talk.

4. _____ fell from the sky.

5. _____ placed the slipper on Cinderella's foot.

6. _____ always makes me cry.

7. _____ disappeared into a black hole.

8. _____ really meant a lot to me.

9. _____ ate five pounds of cherries.

10. _____ lived happily ever after.

B Recognizing Singular and Plural Subjects

The subject of a sentence can be *singular* or *plural*. A **singular subject** is one person, place, or thing.

> Marissa did research on the Internet.

A **plural subject** is more than one person, place, or thing.

> Students often do research on the Internet.

A plural subject that joins two or more subjects with *and* is called a **compound subject**.

> Marissa and Jason did research on the Internet.

PRACTICE 15-4

Each item listed here could be the subject of a sentence. Write *S* after each item that could be a singular subject, and write *P* after each item that could be a plural subject.

Examples

Joey Ramone _____S_____

The Ramones _____P_____

Joey and Johnny Ramone _____P_____

1. hot-fudge sundaes _____

2. the USS *Enterprise* _____

3. life and death _____

4. the McCaughey septuplets _____

5. my Web site _____

6. three blind mice _____

7. Betty and Barney Rubble _____

8. her two children _____

9. Texas _____

10. Ruben Blades _____

PRACTICE 15-5

First, underline the simple subject in each sentence. Then, label each singular subject *S*, and label each plural subject *P*. (Remember that a compound subject is plural.)

> *S*
> **Example:** The Vietnam Veterans <u>Memorial</u> opened to the public on November 11, 1982.

1. The memorial honors men and women killed or missing in the Vietnam War.

2. More than 58,000 names appear on the black granite wall.

3. More than two and a half million people visit the memorial each year.

4. Visitors leave mementoes at the site.

5. Some men and women, for example, leave letters and photographs.

6. Other people leave combat boots, stuffed animals, rosaries, or dog tags.

7. One man leaves a six-pack of beer each year.

8. Visitors also leave cigarettes, flowers, canned food, and clothing.

9. Spouses, children, parents, and friends leave gifts for men and women lost in the war.

10. A Persian Gulf War veteran left his medal for his father.

C Identifying Prepositional Phrases

As you have seen, every sentence includes a subject and a verb. As you try to identify sentence subjects, you may be confused by prepositional phrases, which include nouns or pronouns.

A **prepositional phrase** is made up of a **preposition** (a word like *on, to, in,* or *with*) and its **object** (the noun or pronoun it introduces).

Preposition	+	*Object*	=	*Prepositional Phrase*
on		the roof		on the roof
to		Leah's apartment		to Leah's apartment
in		my Spanish class		in my Spanish class
with		her		with her

Because the object of a preposition is a noun or a pronoun, it may look like the subject of a sentence. However, the object of a preposition can never be a subject. To identify a sentence's subject, cross out all the prepositional phrases. (Remember, every prepositional phrase is introduced by a preposition.)

SUBJECT —————————— PREPOSITIONAL PHRASES ——————————

The <u>price</u> ~~of a new home in the San Francisco Bay area~~ is very high.

Frequently Used Prepositions

about	behind	for	off	toward
above	below	from	on	under
across	beneath	in	onto	underneath
after	beside	including	out	until
against	between	inside	outside	up
along	beyond	into	over	upon
among	by	like	through	with
around	despite	near	throughout	within
at	during	of	to	without
before	except			

▓ PRACTICE 15-6 ▓

Each of the sentences in the following paragraph includes at least one prepositional phrase. To identify each sentence's subject—the noun or pronoun that the sentence is about—first cross out every prepositional phrase. Then, underline the simple subject.

Example: Sudoku <u>puzzles</u> are popular ~~around the world~~.

(1) People are wild about sudoku puzzles. (2) They can be full of

challenges. (3) Each puzzle consists of nine 3x3 squares. (4) A player must write numbers in the squares. (5) However, each number may appear only once in each column, each row, and each 3x3 square. (6) The level of difficulty of each puzzle is determined by the "givens." (7) The "givens" of an individual puzzle make that puzzle unique. (8) Mathematicians with an interest in sudoku have discovered over five billion unique grids. (9) However, solvers of these puzzles are not usually mathematicians. (10) In fact, sudoku players do not need an expert knowledge of math.

D Identifying Action Verbs

An **action verb** tells what the subject does, did, or will do.

> Kobe Bryant <u>plays</u> basketball.
> Columbus <u>sailed</u> across the ocean.
> Andrea <u>will go</u> to Houston next month.

Action verbs can also show mental or emotional action.

> Nirav often <u>thinks</u> about his future.
> Wendy <u>loves</u> backpacking.

When the subject of a sentence performs more than one action, the sentence includes two or more action verbs.

> Lois <u>left</u> work, <u>drove</u> to Somerville, and <u>met</u> Carmen for dinner.

PRACTICE 15-7

In each of the following sentences, underline each action verb twice. (Some sentences include more than one action verb.)

Example: Many nineteenth-century Americans <u>left</u> their homes and <u>journeyed</u> to unfamiliar places.

(1) During the 1840s, thousands of Americans traveled west to places like Oregon, Nevada, and California. (2) Many travelers began their journey in Independence, Missouri. (3) In towns all around Missouri, travelers advertised in newspapers for strong young companions for the journey west. (4) Thousands of wagons eventually departed from

Independence on the dangerous four-month trip to California. (5) Whole families packed their bags and joined wagon trains. (6) The wagons carried food, supplies, and weapons. (7) Some travelers wrote letters to friends and relatives back east. (8) Others wrote in journals. (9) In these letters and journals, we see the travelers' fear and misery. (10) Traveling 2,500 miles west across plains, deserts, and mountains, many people suffered and died.

■ PRACTICE 15-8

Write an action verb in each space to show what action the subject is, was, or will be performing.

Example: I ___drove___ my car to the grocery store.

1. Good athletes sometimes _____ but often _____.

2. After opening the letter, Michele _____.

3. The dolphin _____ and _____ on top of the waves.

4. Thousands of people _____ in the storm.

5. The computer _____, _____, and died.

6. The hurricane _____ the residents and _____ the town.

7. Smoke _____ out of the windows.

8. The Doberman _____.

9. A voice _____ from the balcony.

10. Wanda _____ the door.

STRATEGIES FOR COLLEGE SUCCESS

Spotting Key Words on Essay Exams

When you read an essay exam question, look for key words that tell you how to approach the question. For example, are you being asked to "argue," "analyze," "summarize," "give examples," or do something else? For additional tips on how to become a successful student, see Chapter 1.

E Identifying Linking Verbs

A **linking verb** does not show action. Instead, it connects the subject to a word or words that describe or rename it. The linking verb tells what the subject is (or what it was, seems to be, or will be).

SUBJECT LINKING VERB WORDS THAT DESCRIBE SUBJECT

Calculus is a difficult course.

Many linking verbs, such as *is*, are forms of the verb *be*. Other linking verbs refer to the senses (*look, feel, seem,* and so on).

Tremaine looks very handsome today.
Time seemed to pass quickly.

Frequently Used Linking Verbs

act	become	look	sound
appear	feel	remain	taste
be (am, is, are,	get	seem	turn
was, were)	grow	smell	

PRACTICE 15-9

Underline the verb in each of the following sentences twice. Then, in the blank, indicate whether the verb is an action verb (*AV*) or a linking verb (*LV*).

Example: U.S. labor officials <u>predict</u> growth in service jobs through at least 2016. *AV*

1. An aging population is one trend that is creating more service jobs.

   _____

2. For example, older citizens need nursing care and other health services. _____

3. With a home health aide, many elderly people feel confident about staying in their homes instead of moving to a nursing home.

   _____

4. For this reason, home health workers are in demand. _____

5. Related service fields, such as home maintenance, look strong too. _____

6. Also, officials see rapid growth in education services, including teaching._____

7. More and more students today realize the benefits of a college degree. _____

8. Other fast-growing service fields include retail sales and management. _____

9. Consumers seem ready to shop even in tough economic times. _____

10. Customer-service jobs, in fields like information technology and finance, are also likely to experience growth. _____

■ PRACTICE 15-10

In the following sentences, underline each linking verb twice. Then, circle the complete subject and the word or words that describe or rename it.

Example: (The juice) tasted (sour).

1. The night grew cold.

2. The song seems very familiar.

3. In January 2008, Barack H. Obama became the forty-fourth president of the United States.

4. College students feel pressured by their families, their instructors, and their peers.

5. Many people were outraged at the mayor's announcement.

6. The cheese smelled peculiar.

7. The fans appeared upset by their team's defeat.

8. After the game, the crowd turned ugly.

9. Charlie got sick after eating six corn dogs.

10. My love for my dog remains strong and true.

F Identifying Helping Verbs

Many verbs are made up of more than one word. For example, the verb in the following sentence is made up of two words.

Andrew <u>must make</u> a choice.

In this sentence, *make* is the **main verb**, and *must* is a **helping verb**. A sentence's complete verb is made up of the main verb plus all the helping verbs that accompany it.

In each of the following sentences, the complete verb is underlined twice, and the helping verbs are checkmarked.

Ana <u>h̆as worked</u> at the diner for two years.

<u>D̆oes</u> Ana still <u>work</u> at the diner?

Ana <u>d̆oes</u> not <u>work</u> on Saturdays.

Ana <u>c̆an choose</u> her own hours.

Ana <u>m̆ay work</u> this Saturday.

Ana <u>sh̆ould take</u> a vacation this summer.

Ana <u>m̆ust work</u> hard to earn money for college.

Frequently Used Helping Verbs

am	did	has	might	were
are	do	have	must	will
can	does	is	should	would
could	had	may	was	

PRACTICE 15-11

Each of these sentences includes one or more helping verbs as well as a main verb. Underline the complete verb (the main verb and all the helping verbs) in each sentence twice. Then, put a check mark above each helping verb.

Example: Elizabeth II <u>h̆as been</u> queen of England since 1952.

1. Obese adolescents may risk serious health problems as adults.

2. The candidates will name their running mates within two weeks.

3. Henry has been thinking about changing careers for a long time.

4. Do you want breakfast now?

5. I could have been a French major.

6. This must be the place.

7. I have often wondered about my family's history.

8. You should have remembered the mustard.

9. Jenelle has always loved animals.

10. Research really does take a long time.

✓ Seeing and Writing: Skills Check

Look back at your response to the Seeing and Writing activity on page 217. Reread it carefully, and then complete the following tasks:

- Underline the simple subject of every sentence once.
- Underline the complete verb (the main verb plus all the helping verbs) of every sentence twice.
- Circle the main verb in each sentence, and put a check mark above each helping verb.

Now, revise and edit your paragraph.

The Triangle Shirtwaist Company fire

CHAPTER REVIEW

EDITING PRACTICE

Read the following paragraph. Underline the simple subject of each sentence once, and underline the complete verb twice. To help you locate the subject, cross out the prepositional phrases. The first sentence has been done for you.

The Triangle Shirtwaist Company Fire

~~On March 25, 1911~~, a terrible <u>event</u> <u>revealed</u> the unsafe conditions ~~in factories across the United States~~. On that day, a fire at the Triangle Shirtwaist Company killed 146 workers, mainly young immigrant women. These women could not leave the building during working hours. In fact, the factory owners locked most of the exit doors during the day. On the day of the fire, flames spread quickly through the ten-story building. Workers were trapped behind locked doors. Fire engine ladders could not reach the upper floors. In their terror, some people leaped to their deaths from the burning building. After this tragedy, American

Woman (left) wearing a shirtwaist

labor unions grew stronger. Workers eventually gained the right to a shorter workweek and better working conditions. Today, fire safety is very important at most workplaces. For this reason, a tragedy like the one at the Triangle Shirtwaist Company should never happen again.

COLLABORATIVE ACTIVITIES

1. Working in a group of three or four students, write a subject on a slip of paper. On another slip, write a prepositional phrase; on a third, write an action verb. Fold up the slips, keeping subjects, prepositional phrases, and action verbs in separate piles. Choose one slip from each pile, and use them to create an interesting sentence, adding whatever other words are necessary.

2. Working in a group of three students, have each person list three nouns on a blank sheet of paper and pass the paper to the next student, who should add a verb beside each noun. Then, have the third person add a prepositional phrase that can complete each sentence. Each student should then label the subject, verb, and prepositional phrase in the three sentences he or she has completed.

3. *Composing original sentences* Work with another student to create five simple sentences on a topic of your choice. Make sure each sentence contains a subject and a verb. When you have finished, check your sentences to make sure each sentence begins with a capital letter and ends with a period.

✓ Review Checklist

Writing Simple Sentences

☐ The subject tells who or what is being talked about in the sentence. (See 15A.)

☐ A subject can be singular or plural. (See 15B.)

☐ The object of a preposition cannot be the subject of a sentence. (See 15C.)

☐ An action verb tells what the subject does, did, or will do. (See 15D.)

☐ A linking verb connects the subject to a word or words that describe or rename the subject. (See 15E.)

☐ Many verbs are made up of more than one word—a main verb and one or more helping verbs. (See 15F.)

Writing Compound Sentences

PREVIEW

In this chapter, you will learn

- to form compound sentences with coordinating conjunctions (**16A**)
- to form compound sentences with semicolons (**16B**)
- to form compound sentences with transitional words and phrases (**16C**)

WORD POWER

unique: the only one; one of a kind

classic: an outstanding example of its kind

SEEING AND WRITING ▲

The picture above shows a car that is truly one of a kind. Suppose you wanted to sell this car. Study the picture carefully, and then write a paragraph in which you describe the car in a way that would make someone want to buy it. Try to use the Word Power words in your paragraph.

The most basic kind of sentence, a **simple sentence**, consists of a single **independent clause**—one <u>subject</u> and one <u>verb</u>.

> Many college <u>students</u> <u>major</u> in psychology.
> Many other <u>students</u> <u>major</u> in business.

A **compound sentence** is made up of two or more simple sentences (independent clauses).

A Using Coordinating Conjunctions

One way to create a compound sentence is by joining two simple sentences with a **coordinating conjunction** preceded by a comma.

> Many college students major in psychology, but many other students major in business.

Coordinating Conjunctions		
and	nor	so
but	or	yet
for		

PRACTICE 16-1

Each of the following compound sentences is made up of two simple sentences joined by a coordinating conjunction. Underline the coordinating conjunction in each compound sentence. Then, bracket the two simple sentences. Remember that each simple sentence includes a subject and a verb.

Example: [I do not like unnecessary delays], <u>nor</u> [do I like lame excuses].

1. Speech is silver, but silence is golden.

2. I fought the law, and the law won.

3. The house was dark, so she didn't ring the doorbell.

4. He decided to sign the contract, for he did not want to lose the job.

5. They will not surrender, and they will not agree to a cease-fire.

6. I could order the chicken fajitas, or I could have chili.

7. She has lived in California for years, yet she remembers her childhood in Kansas very clearly.

8. Professor Blakemore was interesting, but Professor Salazar was inspiring.

9. Melody dropped French, and she signed up for Italian.

10. Give me liberty, or give me death.

Coordinating conjunctions join two ideas of equal importance.

Idea (Simple Sentence)	+	Coordinating Conjunction	+	Idea (Simple Sentence)	=	Compound Sentence
Brenda is a vegetarian	+	but	+	Larry eats everything	=	Brenda is a vegetarian, but Larry eats everything.

Coordinating conjunctions describe the relationship between the two ideas, showing how and why the ideas are connected. Different coordinating conjunctions have different meanings:

- To indicate addition, use *and*.

    Edgar Allan Poe wrote horror fiction in the nineteenth century, and Stephen King writes horror fiction today.

- To indicate contrast or contradiction, use *but* or *yet*.

    Poe wrote short stories, but King writes both stories and novels.
    Poe died young, yet his stories live on.

- To indicate a cause-and-effect connection, use *so* or *for*.

    I liked *Carrie*, so I decided to read King's other novels.

    Poe's "The Tell-Tale Heart" is a chilling tale, for it is about a horrible murder.

- To present alternatives, use *or*.

    I have to finish *Cujo*, or I won't be able to sleep.

- To eliminate alternatives, use *nor*.

    I have not read *The Green Mile*, nor have I seen the movie.

FOCUS

Using Commas with Coordinating Conjunctions

When you use a coordinating conjunction to join two simple sentences into a compound sentence, always place a comma before the coordinating conjunction.

We can see a movie, or we can go to a club.

PRACTICE 16-2

Fill in the coordinating conjunction—*and, but, for, nor, or, so,* or *yet*—that most logically links the two parts of each of the following compound sentences.

Example: The meteorologist predicted sun, ___*so*___ we planned a trip

to the beach.

1. Katya does not eat meat, _____ does she eat dairy products.

2. Malik planned to stay single, _____ then he met Alyssa.

3. The Russells wanted to save money on their heating bill, _____ they

   sealed cracks around their windows.

4. Some students buy textbooks online, _____ prices may be lower

   there than in the campus bookstore.

5. Campers can stay in wooden cabins, _____ they can sleep in their

   own tents.

6. Dexter is an excellent cook, _____ he never cleans up the kitchen.

7. Every morning, Alessandro goes to the gym, _____ his wife works

   out at home with Wii Fit.

8. Tony hates the sight of blood, _____ his favorite shows are crime

   dramas.

9. On Sunday afternoons, I work around the house, _____ I relax in

   the back yard.

10. Good used cars can be inexpensive, _____ they often cost less to

    insure than new cars.

PRACTICE 16-3

Fill in the coordinating conjunction—*and, but, for, nor, or, so,* or *yet*—that most logically links the two parts of each of the compound sentences in the following paragraph.

Example: Three teenagers met in Newark, New Jersey, ___*and*___ they

made a pact to beat the odds.

(1) George Jenkins, Sampson Davis, and Rameck Hunt agreed to go to college to become doctors, ———— they promised to help each other succeed. (2) The odds were against them, ———— they lived in inner-city neighborhoods devastated by drugs and violence. (3) They did not have many opportunities, ———— did they have many positive role models. (4) Two of them were involved in crime, ———— one spent time in jail. (5) Fortunately, all three were accepted at University High, a school for gifted students, ———— they never would have met one another. (6) They did not make a big deal of their pact, ———— they all took it seriously. (7) None of them wanted to disappoint the others, ———— they all worked hard to make their dream a reality. (8) The young men's success was a result of their intelligence and determination, ———— it was also a result of their loyal friendship. (9) Jenkins, Davis, and Hunt hoped that their story would inspire others, ———— they wrote a book called *The Pact* about their promise. (10) They also started The Three Doctors Foundation, ———— they wanted to create opportunities for inner-city youths.

PRACTICE 16-4

Using the coordinating conjunctions provided, add a complete independent clause to each sentence in the following pairs to create two different compound sentences. Remember that each coordinating conjunction indicates a different relationship between ideas.

Example

They married at age eighteen, and _they had ten children_____.

They married at age eighteen, so _they had to grow up together_____.

1. Adoption is a complex and emotional process, so _____

_____.

Adoption is a complex and emotional process, but _____

_____.

2. Drunk drivers should lose their licenses, for _____

_____.

Drunk drivers should lose their licenses, or _____

_____.

3. A smoke-free environment has many advantages, and _____

_____.

A smoke-free environment has many advantages, but _____

_____.

4. Female pilots have successfully flown combat missions, yet _____

_____.

Female pilots have successfully flown combat missions, so _____

_____.

5. The death penalty can be abolished, or _____

_____.

The death penalty should not be abolished, nor _____

_____.

PRACTICE 16-5

Add coordinating conjunctions to combine the sentences in the following
paragraph where necessary to relate one idea to another. Remember to
put a comma before each coordinating conjunction that you add.

Example: Americans love the freedom and independence of driving a
, and they
car/~~They~~ also love movies.
^

(1) Drive-in movies were a popular form of entertainment in the
1950s. (2) Today, only a few drive-ins remain. (3) Not surprisingly, the
United States was the home of the first drive-in movie theater. (4) The
first drive-in opened in New Jersey in 1934. (5) The second one, Shankweiler's Drive-In in Orefield, Pennsylvania, opened the same year.
(6) Today, the first drive-in no longer exists. (7) There are not many
other drive-in theaters in New Jersey. (8) However, Shankweiler's is still

open for business. (9) Fans of drive-ins can still go there. (10) Shankweiler's Drive-In still has the in-car speakers that moviegoers used to hang in their car windows. (11) They are rarely used. (12) Instead, drive-in visitors simply turn on the car radio to hear the movie sound. (13) Shankweiler's broadcasts movie soundtracks on FM stereo. (14) Anyone with a car, a love of movies, and a sense of history should make a trip to Shankweiler's Drive-In.

■ PRACTICE 16-6

Add coordinating conjunctions to combine sentences where necessary to relate one idea to another. Remember to put a comma before each coordinating conjunction that you add.

>   *, but dating*
> **Example:** In India, some people look for their own mates/~~Dating~~ is not
>   ^
>   widespread there.

(1) Arranged marriages may seem old-fashioned to some. (2) They are very important in India. (3) In fact, "love matches," or nonarranged marriages, are often seen as unlucky. (4) Many Indians prefer arranged marriages. (5) The matchmaking process can vary. (6) The following steps are typical. (7) First, the parents of a single man or woman put out the word that their child is available. (8) Then, the parents gather information about potential mates. (9) They consider this information carefully. (10) Factors that parents examine include the potential mate's profession, educational background, and horoscope. (11) At this point, either set of parents may find a potential spouse unacceptable. (12) The process may stop. (13) Otherwise, the parents will meet to learn more about one another and their potential son-in-law or daughter-in-law. (14) In Japan, arranged marriage—known as *omiai*—is less common than it is in India. (15) It still occurs. (16) A go-between, or *nakodo*, helps to make the match. (17) The man and woman matched by a nakodo meet. (18) They may decide to pursue a relationship. (19) They do not

have to follow the nakodo's advice. (20) They do not feel pressured to dismiss it. (21) People who are busy or shy especially appreciate a nakodo's help. (22) He can save them from the time-consuming and awkward process of finding a mate.

PRACTICE 16-7

Write an original compound sentence on each of the following topics. Use the coordinating conjunction provided, and remember to put a comma before the coordinating conjunction in each compound sentence.

Example: *Topic:* course requirements
Coordinating conjunction: but

Composition is a required course for all first-year students, but biology is

not required.

1. *Topic:* rising college tuition
Coordinating conjunction: so

_____

_____

2. *Topic:* interracial families
Coordinating conjunction: but

_____

_____

3. *Topic:* two things you hate to do
Coordinating conjunction: and

_____

_____

4. *Topic:* why you made a certain decision
Coordinating conjunction: for

_____

_____

5. *Topic:* something you regret
Coordinating conjunction: yet

_____

_____

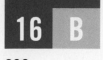

6. *Topic:* two possible career choices
Coordinating conjunction: or

_____

_____

7. *Topic:* two household chores you would rather not do
Coordinating conjunction: nor

_____

_____

B Using Semicolons

Another way to create a compound sentence is by joining two simple sentences (independent clauses) with a **semicolon**.

> The Democrats held their convention in Boston; the Republicans held their convention in New York.

FOCUS

Avoiding Sentence Fragments

A semicolon can join two complete sentences. It cannot join a sentence and a fragment.

INCORRECT ⎡——————————— FRAGMENT ———————————⎤
Because New York City has excellent public transportation; it was a good choice for the convention.

CORRECT New York City has excellent public transportation; it was a good choice for the convention.

For more on identifying and correcting sentence fragments, see Chapter 21.

PRACTICE 16-8

Each of the following items consists of a simple sentence followed by a semicolon. For each item, add another simple sentence to create a compound sentence.

Example: Some people love to watch sports on television; *others*

would rather play a game than watch one.

1. Baseball is known as "America's pastime"; _____
_____.

2. The most-played sport in the United States is probably basketball; ____
_____.

3. Soccer has gained popularity in recent years; _____
_____.

4. American football requires size and strength; _____
_____.

5. Professional sports teams usually give their fans something to cheer
about; _____
_____.

6. The Olympic Games honor athletes from around the world; _____
_____.

7. Individual Olympic athletes compete in events such as track and
field; _____
_____.

8. Some athletes are models of good sportsmanship; _____
_____.

9. A good coach knows how to encourage an athlete; _____
_____.

10. Many children admire sports heroes; _____
_____.

STRATEGIES FOR COLLEGE SUCCESS

Using the Internet to Answer Grammar Questions

If grammar questions come up as you write, try looking on
the Internet for answers. For example, you might try *The Online
English Grammar* at edunet.com/English/grammar. For additional
tips on how to become a successful student, see Chapter 1.

C Using Transitional Words and Phrases

Another way to create a compound sentence is by joining two simple sentences with a **transitional word or phrase**. When a transitional word or phrase joins two sentences, a semicolon always comes *before* the transitional word or phrase, and a comma always comes *after* it.

> Women's pro basketball games are often sold out; however, not many people watch the games on television.

> Soccer has become very popular in the United States; in fact, more American children play soccer than any other sport.

Frequently Used Transitional Words

also	however	otherwise
besides	instead	still
consequently	later	subsequently
eventually	meanwhile	then
finally	moreover	therefore
furthermore	nevertheless	thus

Frequently Used Transitional Phrases

after all	in addition	of course
as a result	in comparison	on the contrary
at the same time	in contrast	that is
for example	in fact	
for instance	in other words	

Different transitional words and phrases convey different meanings:

- Some transitional words and phrases signal addition: *also, besides, furthermore, in addition, moreover,* and so on.

  > Golf can be an expensive sport; besides, it can be hard to find a public golf course.

- Some transitional words and phrases show a cause-and-effect connection: *as a result, therefore, consequently, thus,* and so on.

  > Professional baseball players are bigger and stronger than ever before; therefore, home runs have become more common.

- Some transitional words and phrases indicate contradiction or contrast: *nevertheless, however, in contrast, still,* and so on.

  > Some of the world's best athletes are track stars; nevertheless, few of their names are widely known.

- Some transitional words and phrases present alternatives: *instead, on the contrary, otherwise,* and so on.

> Shawn got a football scholarship; otherwise, he could not have gone to college.
> He didn't make the first team; instead, he backed up other players.

- Some transitional words and phrases indicate time sequence: *at the same time, eventually, finally, later, meanwhile, subsequently, then,* and so on.

> The popularity of women's tennis has been growing; meanwhile, the popularity of men's tennis has been declining.

PRACTICE 16-9

Each item below consists of a simple sentence followed by a semicolon and a transitional word or phrase. For each item, add an independent clause to create a complete compound sentence.

Example: Shopping malls appear throughout the country; in fact, *they have replaced many main streets.*

1. Nearly every community is near one or more shopping malls; as a result, _____

2. Some malls include hundreds of stores; moreover, _____

3. Malls include restaurants as well as stores; therefore, _____

4. Some malls serve as social centers; in fact, _____

5. Shopping at malls offers many advantages over traditional shopping; however, _____

6. Malls offer many employment opportunities; for example, _____

_____

_____.

7. Malls provide a safe, climate-controlled atmosphere; nevertheless, ___

_____

_____.

8. Many stores seem to have similar merchandise; in addition, _____

_____

_____.

9. The Mall of America, in Minnesota, even includes an amusement

park; therefore, _____

_____.

10. Some people think malls are wonderful; still, _____

_____

_____.

▉ PRACTICE 16-10 ▉

In each of the following sentences, underline the transitional word or
phrase that joins the two independent clauses. Then, add a semicolon
and a comma to set off each transitional word or phrase.

Example: Most Americans see the one-room schoolhouse as a thing

of the past;however,about 400 one-room schools still operate in the

United States.

1. Most one-room schools are in isolated rural areas that is they exist in

places far from towns with large school systems.

2. Montana and Nebraska still have some one-room schools in contrast

more densely populated states do not have any.

3. Most one-room schools have only one teacher and a few students

therefore one room is all they need.

4. The addition of just a few children can cause a school to outgrow its

one room as a result the town may have to build a larger school.

5. These days, declining population is the reason most one-room schools close in other words the town does not have enough students to make operating the school worthwhile.

6. Running a one-room school can be expensive consequently many rural communities share a larger school with nearby towns.

7. Supporters of one-room schools see many benefits for example students in these schools get a lot of individual attention from their teachers.

8. One-room schools tend to produce confident, thoughtful students moreover these students tend to do well on state-wide tests.

9. One-room schools also give a town's residents a sense of community and tradition therefore many towns fight hard to keep their schools.

10. So far, the Croydon Village School in New Hampshire has managed to keep its doors open still residents do not take their school for granted.

PRACTICE 16-11

Consulting the lists of transitional words and phrases on page 240, choose a word or expression that logically connects each pair of sentences below into one compound sentence. Be sure to punctuate appropriately.

Example: Temporary memorials along roadways are a familiar sight
; however, some
these days/~~Some~~ people find them distracting and even dangerous.
^

1. Many memorials honor the victims of car accidents. Locating them along the roadways makes sense.

2. Some memorials are nearly invisible. Some are almost impossible to miss.

3. A memorial is sometimes just a simple white cross. People often add flowers, photos, toys, or teddy bears.

4. No one wants victims to be forgotten. These memorials can cause problems.

WORD POWER

shrine: a place at which respects are paid to a person who has died

5. The memorials can create obstacles for snowplows and lawnmowers. They can distract curious drivers.

6. Delaware has taken steps to limit the number of memorials on its roads. Officials want mourners to use an established memorial park.

7. This seems to be a sensible compromise. It does not address one essential issue.

8. The exact location of the victim's death is important to mourners. Mourners sometimes put themselves in danger to reach the right spot.

9. Most states do not enforce their regulations about temporary memorials. some memorials remain beside roads for many months.

10. A public outlet for people's grief is clearly needed. This debate is likely to continue.

■ PRACTICE 16-12

Using the specified topics and transitional words or phrases, create five compound sentences. Be sure to punctuate correctly.

Example: *Topic:* popular music
Transitional word: nevertheless

Many popular singing groups today seem to have been put together by a

committee; nevertheless, many of these groups sell millions of records.

1. *Topic:* finding a job
Transitional phrase: for example

_____

_____

2. *Topic:* gun safety
Transitional word: otherwise

_____

_____

3. *Topic:* abstinence
Transitional phrase: as a result

_____

_____

4. *Topic:* credit-card debt
   Transitional word: still

_____

_____

5. *Topic:* watching television
   Transitional word: however

_____

_____

✓ Seeing and Writing: Skills Check

Look back at your response to the Seeing and Writing activity on page 230. Reread it, underlining every compound sentence. Then, answer the following questions:

- Have you used the coordinating conjunction or transitional word or phrase that best communicates your meaning?
- Have you punctuated these sentences correctly?

Make any necessary changes.

Now, look for a pair of short simple sentences in your writing that you could combine, and use one of the three methods discussed in this chapter to join them into one compound sentence.
   Finally, revise and edit your paragraph.

CHAPTER REVIEW

EDITING PRACTICE

Read the following student paragraph. Then, create compound sentences by linking pairs of simple sentences where appropriate. You can join sentences with a coordinating conjunction, a semicolon, or a transitional word or phrase. Remember to put commas before coordinating conjunctions that join two simple sentences and to use semicolons and commas correctly with transitional words and phrases. The first two sentences have been combined for you.

A man playing quad rugby

Murderball Slays Stereotypes

The 2005 documentary *Murderball* introduced many people to an unfamiliar
   ; at the same time, it
sport/It helped change people's views of disabled athletes. Most audiences had
   ^

never heard of quadriplegic rugby. They were not prepared for the full-contact nature

Quad rugby players

of the sport. In quad rugby, players in wheelchairs smash into one another. They often fall out of their chairs. For many viewers, this is difficult to watch. Physically disabled people are usually seen as fragile. *Murderball* tells a different story. The players clearly love the roughness of the game. They refuse to wear pads, helmets, or other protective gear. The audience is not allowed to pity these players. The audience is encouraged to admire them and their fast-paced, demanding sport. Quad rugby is exciting to watch. Spectators are easily caught up in the game. The players are also highly competitive, strong, and even arrogant. They resemble many able-bodied professional athletes. For player Mark Zupan, this resemblance is key. He does not want the emphasis to be on the players' disabilities. He wants people to recognize their abilities. The movie *Murderball* makes people do just that.

COLLABORATIVE ACTIVITIES

1. Working in pairs, use a coordinating conjunction to join each sentence in the left-hand column below with a sentence in the right-hand column to create ten compound sentences. Use as many different coordinating conjunctions as you can to connect ideas. Be sure each coordinating conjunction you choose conveys a logical relationship between ideas, and remember to put a comma before each one. You may use some of the listed sentences more than once. (Many different combinations—some serious and factually accurate, some humorous—are possible.)

Miniskirts get shorter every year.	Some come with a belt.
Those shoes are an ugly color.	They are torn and dirty.
Berries usually ripen in the summer.	My mother hates them.
Wild mushrooms grow all over the world.	Some kinds are edible.
I bought seven pairs of earrings.	The silver ones are my favorites.
His pants are dragging on the ground.	Only experts should pick them.
Everyone at work has to wear a uniform.	Digging them up is my job.
The yard is full of dandelions.	I will not try them on.
Ostrich eggs are enormous.	I love to throw them in salads.
Cherry tomatoes make excellent snacks.	Each one could make several omelettes.

2. Working in a group of three or four students, invent a new sport. Begin by writing one rule of the game in the form of a simple sentence. Then, pass the paper to the person on your right. That person should expand the rule into a compound sentence.

Example

ORIGINAL RULE   The ball must not touch the ground.

CHANGED RULE   The ball must not touch the ground; moreover, the players can only move the ball with their elbows.

Keep going until you have five complete rules. Then, work together to write additional sentences describing the playing area, teams, uniforms, or anything else about your new sport. Use compound sentences whenever possible.

3. *Composing original sentences*   Work with another student to create six compound sentences. Make sure that each compound sentence includes two simple sentences, each with a subject and a verb. Two of your sentences should join clauses with coordinating conjunctions, two with semicolons, and two with transitional words or phrases. When you have finished, check your sentences to make sure you have punctuated them correctly.

✓ Review Checklist

Writing Compound Sentences

☐ A compound sentence is made up of two simple sentences (independent clauses).

☐ A coordinating conjunction—*and, but, for, nor, or, so,* or *yet*—can join two simple sentences into one compound sentence. A comma always comes before the coordinating conjunction. (See 16A.)

☐ A semicolon can join two simple sentences into one compound sentence. (See 16B.)

☐ A transitional word or phrase can join two simple sentences into one compound sentence. When it joins two sentences, a transitional word or phrase is always preceded by a semicolon and followed by a comma. (See 16C.)

Writing Complex Sentences

SEEING AND WRITING ▲

Look at the picture above, which shows an elementary school class picture. Then, write a paragraph about the childhood friends you've lost touch with. Why do you think you don't see these friends anymore? Which, if any, would you like to see again? Try to use the Word Power words in your paragraph.

A **complex sentence** is made up of one independent clause and one or more dependent clauses.

```
                                          ┌─ INDEPENDENT ─┐
COMPLEX SENTENCE   Because Tanya was sick yesterday, I had to work
                   └ CLAUSE ──────────────┘
                   a double shift.
```

Note that sometimes the independent clause comes first in a complex sentence:

> I had to work a double shift because Tanya was sick today.

A Using Subordinating Conjunctions

You can create a complex sentence by joining two simple sentences (independent clauses). Add a **subordinating conjunction**—a word like *although* or *because*—to one of the sentences, turning it into a dependent clause.

TWO SENTENCES   The election was close. The state supreme court did not order a recount.

```
                  ┌────── DEPENDENT CLAUSE ──────┐ ┌───── INDEPENDENT ─────┐
COMPLEX SENTENCE  Although the election was close, the state supreme court
                  └ CLAUSE ───────────────────────┘
                  did not order a recount.
```

Keep in mind that once you add a subordinating conjunction to a simple sentence, it can no longer stand alone. It needs an independent clause to complete its meaning.

Frequently Used Subordinating Conjunctions

after	if only	till
although	in order that	unless
as	now that	until
as if	once	when
as though	provided	whenever
because	rather than	where
before	since	whereas
even if	so that	wherever
even though	than	whether
if	though	while

PRACTICE 17-1

Write an appropriate subordinating conjunction on each blank line
below. Consult the list of subordinating conjunctions on page 249
to make sure you choose one that establishes a logical relationship
between ideas. (The required punctuation has been provided.)

Example: _____*If*_____ you were alive in the early part of the twentieth century, you probably saw a vaudeville show.

(1) _____ there was film, radio, or television, people needed other
forms of entertainment. (2) Vaudeville shows were a popular choice in the
late nineteenth and early twentieth centuries _____ you lived in a city.
(3) _____ vaudeville shows were variety shows with many different
acts, they usually offered something for everyone. (4) Audiences could
often see comedians, mind readers, and escape artists as well as singers
and dancers _____ they went to a vaudeville show. (5) The "headliner,"
the biggest star, usually performed next to last _____ a less-popular per-
former went last. (6) _____ they could draw big crowds, theaters used
colorful posters to advertise their headliners. (7) Large audiences were sure
to appear _____ the schedule featured comedians Eddie Cantor and
W.C. Fields, actresss Sarah Bernhardt, or piano player Eubie Blake.
(8) _____ many individual performers were popular, some family
acts like the Four Cohans, the Dolly Sisters, and the Three Keatons also
had fans. (9) Fortunately, audiences did not lose their beloved performers
_____ vaudeville began to decline in the 1920s. (10) For example, _____
vaudeville became a thing of the past, George Burns and Gracie Allen
became internationally famous comedians on the radio. (11) Moreover,
_____ talking movies became available in the late 1920s, fans could see
and hear many of their favorite vaudeville stars on screen.

PRACTICE 17-2

Complete each of the following complex sentences by finishing the
dependent clause on the line provided.

Example: Some students succeed in school because _*they have good*_
*study habits.* .

1. After _____, these students review their lecture notes and reread the assignment.

2. They memorize facts from their notes even though _____ _____.

3. Sometimes these students copy key facts from lectures onto note cards so that _____.

4. Teachers sometimes give surprise quizzes because _____ _____.

5. Students might do poorly on these quizzes unless _____ _____.

6. Even if _____, they are prepared for the unexpected.

7. Whenever _____, good students ask questions to be sure they understand the assignment.

8. When _____, good students begin their research early.

9. They narrow the topic and develop a tentative thesis before _____ _____.

10. Since _____, good students are always prepared.

STRATEGIES FOR COLLEGE SUCCESS
Creating Your Own Work Space

You probably already have a work space in your bedroom or dorm room. If this space is missing something that would make your work easier—such as good lighting, a comfortable chair, or storage for supplies—make the change now. For additional tips on how to become a successful student, see Chapter 1.

Punctuating with Subordinating Conjunctions

To punctuate a complex sentence that contains a subordinating conjunction, follow these rules:

■ Use a comma after the dependent clause.

┌───────────────── DEPENDENT CLAUSE ─────────────────┐ ┌──────
Although they had no formal training as engineers, Orville and
┌───────── INDEPENDENT CLAUSE ─────────┐
Wilber Wright built the first airplane.

■ Do not use a comma after the independent clause.

┌──────────────── INDEPENDENT CLAUSE ────────────────┐
Orville and Wilber Wright built the first airplane although they had
┌───────── DEPENDENT CLAUSE ─────────┐
no formal training as engineers.

■ PRACTICE 17-3

Some of the following complex sentences are punctuated correctly, and some are not. Put a *C* next to every sentence that is punctuated correctly. If the punctuation is not correct, edit the sentence to correct it.

Example: Skateboarding has come a long way since the first commercial boards became available in the 1950s. __*C*__

1. Teenagers used to skate wherever they could find a tempting stretch of concrete. _____

2. When a drought hit southern California in the 1970s homeowners had to leave their pools empty. _____

3. While they were away, daring groups of teenagers trespassed into their back yards. _____

4. The teens skateboarded along the sides of the pool, as if the walls were concrete waves. _____

5. As skateparks became more common, the sport lost some of its bad-boy character. _____

6. Now that skateboarding is more popular skating gear has become fashionable. _____

7. While skaters used to wear slip-on Van shoes, they now wear sneakers. _____

8. Old-time skaters liked loose pants, because the relaxed fit offered freedom of movement. _____

9. Whether they know it or not teens wearing baggy pants today are following a skater trend. _____

10. Although some old-time skaters are disappointed by the mainstream appeal of skateboarding, others are excited about their sport's influence on our culture. _____

PRACTICE 17-4

Combine each of the following pairs of sentences to form one complex sentence, using the subordinating conjunction that follows each pair. Make sure you include a comma where one is required.

Example: ~~People~~ *Even though people* fear deadly viruses such as Ebola/~~Not~~ *, not* enough has been done to provide medical supplies to health-care workers in Africa. (even though)

1. Many Westerners hardly ever think about problems in Africa. The lack of medical supplies should concern everyone. (although)

2. Diseases in African countries often spread. Hospitals and medical personnel there do not have enough equipment. (because)

3. An outbreak of Ebola virus occurred in the Democratic Republic of Congo in 2009. Angola closed part of its border with this country to prevent the spread of the disease. (when)

4. Aid organizations arrived with disinfectant, gloves, and surgical masks. Local medical workers worried about their ability to control the disease. (until)

5. Ebola spreads. Bodily fluids from an infected person come into contact with the skin of a healthy person. (whenever)

6. The Ebola virus makes a patient bleed heavily. Medical workers are in danger. (because)

7. Health-care workers must wear gloves. Their skin never touches the skin of their patients. (so that)

8. At first doctors and nurses in the Democratic Republic of Congo did not have the right equipment to handle the outbreak. They did their best to control it. (even though)

9. International organizations arrived with "Ebola kits" containing protective clothing. Health-care workers were able to aid the sick without fear of infection. (when)

10. Wealthier nations should help poorer countries stockpile supplies. Local medical workers can respond effectively as soon as an outbreak occurs. (so that)

▨ PRACTICE 17-5 ▨

Use each of the subordinating conjunctions below in an original complex sentence. Make sure you punctuate your sentences correctly.

Example

subordinating conjunction: even though

My little sister finally agreed to go to kindergarten even though she was

afraid.

1. *subordinating conjunction:* because

_____

_____

2. *subordinating conjunction:* after

_____

_____

3. *subordinating conjunction:* even if

_____

_____

4. *subordinating conjunction:* until

_____

_____

5. *subordinating conjunction:* whenever

_____

_____

C Using Relative Pronouns

You can also create a complex sentence by joining two simple sentences (independent clauses) with a **relative pronoun** (*who, which, that,* and so on).

TWO SENTENCES   The Miami Heat's LeBron James was the Cleveland Cavaliers' first pick in the 2003 NBA draft. He was only eighteen years old at the time.

COMPLEX SENTENCE   The Miami Heat's LeBron James, who was only eighteen years old at the time, was the Cleveland Cavaliers' first pick in the 2003 NBA draft. (The relative pronoun *who* creates a dependent clause that describes LeBron James.)

Relative Pronouns

that	which	whoever	whomever
what	who	whom	whose

NOTE: *Who* and *whom* always refer to people. *Which* and *that* refer to things.

PRACTICE 17-6

In each of the following complex sentences, underline the dependent clause, and circle the relative pronoun. Then, draw an arrow from the relative pronoun to the noun or pronoun it describes.

Example: Indians (who) wish to maintain their heritage celebrate Diwali, the Festival of Lights.

1. This holiday, which lasts five days, involves special foods, candles, prayers, and presents.

2. The roots of this celebration are in Hinduism, which is one of the oldest religions in the world.

3. Among the special sweets baked for this holiday are cakes that contain saffron, almonds, butter, and milk.

4. Offerings are made to Krishna, who is one of the three main gods of Hinduism.

5. In the evenings, families light candles that stand for the banishing of ignorance and darkness.

6. On the first day of the celebration, people who want good fortune during the coming year decorate their houses with rice flour and red footprints.

7. The second day celebrates a legend about Krishna, who is said to have rescued sixteen thousand daughters of gods and saints from a demon king.

8. The third and most important day consists of feasts, gifts, pilgrimages to temples, and visits to friends whom the family wishes to see.

9. The fourth day, which is associated with legends about mountains, is considered a good day to start a new project.

10. On the last day, families, who meet to exchange gifts, express their love for one another.

■ PRACTICE 17-7

Combine each of the following pairs of sentences into one complex sentence, using the relative pronoun that follows each pair.

Example: Whaling was once an important part of American culture.
, which inspired the great American novel Moby-Dick,
^
~~Whaling inspired the great American novel *Moby-Dick*.~~ (which)

1. In the nineteenth century, American whalers sailed around the world to hunt whales. Their jobs were very dangerous. (whose)

2. Whale oil provided light in many American homes. It burns very brightly. (which)

3. Today, U.S. laws protect several whale species. They are considered to be in danger of extinction. (that)

4. Most Americans approve of the U.S. ban on whaling. They no longer need whale oil for lighting. (who)

5. Whale hunting is the source of a disagreement between the United States and Japan. The two countries have different ideas about whaling. (which)

6. Japanese fleets operate with permission from the International Whaling Commission. The commission allows whales to be killed for scientific research. (which)

7. Japanese merchants are allowed to sell whale meat. This meat is left over after the research. (that)

8. In recent years, the U.S.-based conservation group Sea Shepherd has claimed victories against Japan's whaling industry. The group attempts to disable Japanese whaling ships. (which)

9. The organization has saved hundreds of whales from Japanese harpoons. The organization's activities have been publicized widely. (whose)

10. Sea Shepherd and other groups see the Japanese whale hunt as benefitting not research but businesses. The businesses sell whale meat to restaurants. (that)

PRACTICE 17-8

Complete each of the following items to create a complex sentence. Make sure that each clause of the complex sentence contains a subject and a verb.

Example: A hamburger that *has been barbecued on a grill is one of my favorite things.*

1. When my mother _____

   _____.

2. My best friend, who _____

   _____.

3. If you ever _____

   _____.

4. Although most people _____

   _____.

5. My dream job, which _____

   _____.

✓ Seeing and Writing: Skills Check

Look back at your response to the Seeing and Writing activity on page 248. Reread it, and complete the following tasks:

- Underline every complex sentence.
- Circle the subordinating conjunction or relative pronoun that joins the clauses in each complex sentence.

Now, find a pair of simple sentences that could be combined with a subordinating conjunction or a relative pronoun, and revise the two sentences to create a complex sentence.

Finally, revise and edit the paragraph.

CHAPTER REVIEW

EDITING PRACTICE

Read the following paragraph, and then revise it by using subordinating conjunctions or relative pronouns to combine some simple sentences. Be sure to punctuate correctly. The first revision has been done for you.

The Importance of Birth Order

    Apparently, birth order can affect a child's personality. Oldest children are
            while youngest
achievers/~~Youngest~~ children are free spirits. Oldest children are serious. Youngest
  ^
children like to make people laugh. Families have noticed such differences for